THEMATIC UNIT

Our Legal System

Written by Katie Eyles, M. Ed.

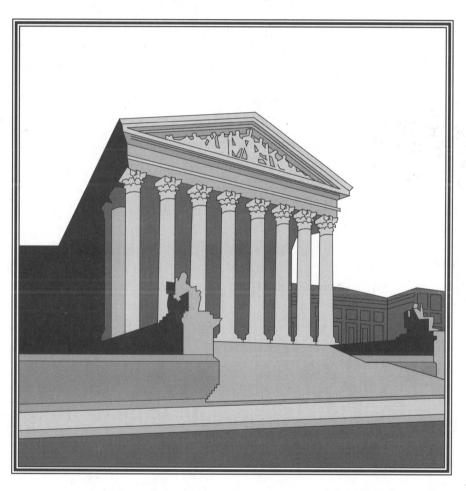

Teacher Created Materials, Inc.
6421 Industry Way
Westminster, CA 92683
www.teachercreated.com
ISBN-1-57690-060-6
©1998 Teacher Created Materials, Inc.
Reprinted, 1999
Made in U.S.A.

Illustrated by
Agi Palinay

Edited by
Walter Kelly, M.A.

Table of Contents

Introduction

Our Legal System is a guide for teachers and students on the basics of the legal system for the United States of America. Through exciting activities such as scavenger hunts, mock trials, mystery puzzles, and vocabulary games, the student learns about concepts of social order, laws, and courtroom procedure. Along with enjoyable activities for students, this unit also provides helpful ideas for teachers: a list of computer software, historical background, creative writing assignments, research assignments, and bulletin board ideas.

The first half of this unit incorporates information about laws, crimes, and the lower courts with new ideas for teaching an old literary classic—Mark Twain's *The Adventures of Tom Sawyer*. The second half of this unit focuses on the Supreme Court, including a biography of the first woman Supreme Court Justice, Sandra Day O'Connor. In both sections, the students learn the basics of our legal system while experiencing a variety of challenging and entertaining activities.

This thematic unit includes the following:

☐ **literature selection**—summary of two books with related lessons that cross the curriculum

☐ **language arts**—suggestions for research and creative writing topics as well as activities on reading comprehension and dialect

☐ **technology**—suggestions for incorporating computer skills within the unit

☐ **bulletin board ideas**—suggestions for student-centered displays

☐ **curriculum connections**—activities to develop skills in language arts, math, science, history, art, drama, and life skills

☐ **bibliography**—a list of additional literature and nonfiction books related to the topic

☐ **group projects and simulations**—methods designed to get the most out of activities with the least amount of confusion in the classroom

---

To keep this valuable resource intact so that it can be used year after year, you may wish to punch holes in the pages and store them in a three-ring binder.

Introduction *(cont.)*

Why a Balanced Approach?

The strength of a whole-language approach is that it involves children in using all modes of communication—reading, writing, listening, observing, illustrating, and doing. Communication skills are interconnected and integrated into lessons that emphasize the whole of language. Balancing this approach is our knowledge that every whole—including individual words—is composed of parts, and directed study of those parts can help a student to master the whole. Experience and research tell us that regular attention to phonics, other word attack skills, spelling, etc., develops reading mastery, thereby fulfilling the unity of the whole language experience. The child is thus led to read, write, spell, speak, and listen confidently in response to a literature experience introduced by the teacher. In these ways, language skills grow rapidly, stimulated by direct practice, involvement, and interest in the topic at hand.

Why Thematic Planning?

One very useful tool for implementing a balanced language program is thematic planning. By choosing a theme with correlating literature selections for a unit of study, a teacher can plan activities throughout the day that lead to a cohesive, in-depth study of the topic. Students will be practicing and applying their skills in meaningful contexts. Consequently, they will tend to learn and retain more. Both teachers and students will be freed from a day that is broken into unrelated segments of isolated drill and practice.

Why Cooperative Learning?

Besides academic skills and content, students need to learn social skills. This area of development cannot be taken for granted. Students must learn to work cooperatively in groups in order to function well in modern society. Group activities should be a regular part of school life, and teachers should consciously include social objectives as well as academic objectives in their planning. For example, a group working together to solve a problem may need to select a leader. Teachers should make clear to the students the qualities of good leader-follower group interaction just as they would state and monitor the academic goals of the project.

Four Basic Components of Cooperative Learning

1. *In cooperative learning, all group members need to work together to accomplish the task.*

2. *Cooperative learning groups should be heterogeneous.*

3. *Cooperative learning activities need to be designed so that each student contributes to the group, and individual group members can be assessed on their performance.*

4. *Cooperative learning teams need to know the social as well as the academic objectives of a lesson.*

The Adventures of Tom Sawyer

by Mark Twain
(HarperCollins, 1997)

Summary

In *The Adventures of Tom Sawyer*, Mark Twain tells a wonderful tale of two mischievous boys growing up in the South. One of the key adventures involves a murder. Late at night when both boys should be in bed, Tom and Huck prowl through the town cemetery, accidentally becoming witnesses to a murder. Swearing secrecy, the two boys watch as an innocent man is jailed for a crime he did not commit. In true Tom-and-Huck fashion, the two decide to run away. Not until the boys realize that the town is mourning their deaths do they reappear. Eventually, Tom decides to break the vow of silence and testify. At risk to his personal safety, he helps an innocent man regain his freedom.

Below is a sample plan for this part of the unit. You may want to modify the plan to meet the needs of your classroom.

Sample Plan

Day 1
- Brainstorm the reasons laws exist.
- Complete the activity on laws. (pages 23–24)
- Read in groups. (Chapters 1–8)
- Complete the Chapter Activities. (pages 44–48)
- Present chapters to the class.
- Discuss Wanted: Samuel Langhorne Clemens. (page 49)

Day 2
- Discuss People in the Courtroom. (page 38)
- Assign Individual Reading. (Chapters 9–10)
- Complete Chapter Activities. (pages 44–48)
- Construct a briefcase. (page 6)

Day 3
- Discuss Chart and Summary of American Court System. (pages 12–14)
- Read in groups chapters 11–23.
- Complete Chapter Activities. (pages 44–48)
- Complete Searching for Terms. (page 17)
- Play Judicial Jargon—Level I. (pages 18 and 19)

Day 4
- Discuss Types of Crimes and Punishments. (page 27)
- Complete Kids and Laws. (page 26)
- Assign Individual Reading. (Chapters 24–25)
- Complete Chapter Activities.
- Play Judicial Jargon—Level II. (pages 20 and 21)

Day 5
- Discuss Motive, Means, and Opportunity. (pages 34 and 35)
- Complete fairy tale crimes. (pages 34 and 35).
- Read Chapters 26–34.
- Complete Chapter Activities. (pages 44–48)
- Read The Mighty Mississippi. (page 50)
- Complete Map of the Mississippi. (page 51)
- Complete Mississippi Math. (page 67)

Day 6
- Begin participation in simulation. (pages 30–36, 65)
- This simulation may actually involve several days of preparation and involvement. The activities include the Drawing of the Crime Scene; the Crime Scene Checklist; Investigation; Motive, Means, and Opportunity; and Suspect Identification Form.

Overview of Activities

Source Books for Our Legal System

This unit is designed to give students a broad scope of the legal system in the United States, how it works, and how the parts fit together. Additional resources may be useful for enrichment activities to answer more specific questions the students may have.

☐ Calvi, James V. *American Law and Legal Systems*. (Prentice Hall, 1992)

This source is a complete guide to the legal system that begins with the history of law and ends with family law.

☐ Deegan, Paul J. *United States Supreme Court Library*. (Abdo & Daughters, 1994)

This source is a short, easy-to-read book about the Supreme Court, including information on famous justices and the court today.

☐ Girfis, Steven H. *Law Dictionary*. (Barron's, 1991)

This book is a handy, large-print dictionary of legal terms.

☐ Hall, Kermit L. *The Oxford Companion to the Supreme Court of the United States*. (Oxford University Press, 1992)

You will find here almost 1,000 pages of everything you ever wanted to know about the Supreme Court.

☐ Kurland, Michael. *How to Solve a Murder: The Forensic Handbook*. (Macmillan, 1995)

This is a fun, reader-friendly forensics guide with examples and trivia that can easily be used in the classroom.

Setting the Stage

Mystery, mayhem, and courtroom drama naturally fascinate students and adults. This unit lends itself to creativity and entertaining activities. The only problem you may encounter is limiting the number of activities you use. Here are a few suggestions for exciting opening activities to set the stage in your classroom.

1. Tell the students that each of them is a world-famous lawyer. If a computer lab is available, ask them to design letterhead stationery for their firm. They should include their name, the name and address of the legal firm, and a logo for their firm. Run off a few pages for each student. Then allow them to write reports or essays on the paper. Make briefcases out of black folders and gold stick-on letters to store papers from the unit.

2. Show students courtroom scenes from mystery shows such as old reruns of *Perry Mason*, *Matlock*, or *LA Law*. Have them identify the defendant, the defense, the prosecuting attorney, the bailiff, and the judge. Ask them to describe what happens in the courtroom.

Overview of Activities *(cont.)*

Setting the Stage *(cont.)*

3. Divide the classroom into groups of three or four. Tell them that they are going to play a new game called "Legal System." Give them unmarked game boards and pieces or decks of cards but no directions. Tell them that the winner of the game gets a prize. When they ask how to play, tell them that they have to decide how the game is played. However, there has to be one winner. Monitor the groups and allow them to play for 5 to 15 minutes. Ask them to stop, move their desks back, and write down what happened. When they finish, ask them to share some of their experiences. Begin a discussion on why we need rules and laws.

4. Read a selection from one of the popular minute mystery books. Give the class five minutes to guess the answer to the mystery. Give the winner a prize.

5. Before class, tape a necklace under one of the student's desks. Give the students a list of clues. The first person to figure out the identity of the criminal receives a reward.

Enjoying Our Legal System

1. Plan two days of dramatic activities using the following activity sheets—**Drawing of the Crime Scene, Crime Scene Checklist, Investigator's Report, Suspect Identification Form, Courtroom Procedure Chart, Options: The Court Case**, and **Fine Arts: Using Drama in the Classroom**. The first day should be The Crime and The Investigation. Give each student an activity to do during the investigation. Assign one person to be the murderer but don't tell the class who that person is. See who can figure out the murderer using the clues. The second day should be The Trial. If the students write the trial, use information collected during the investigation. Tape the activities. Have a movie afternoon with popcorn and soft drinks and invite parents, administrators, and students to view your mystery movie.

2. Use the information in **Newsreel of the 1930s**. Have your own students produce a newsreel of the 1930s to share in history classes.

3. After reading **History of English Laws** and **History of American Legal System**, make a large time line and attach it to one of the classroom walls. Have different students illustrate different events.

4. Decorate the outside of the classroom door to look like the Supreme Court Building.

5. After reading **Ethics—In and Out of Court**, organize panel discussions within the classroom or among members of different classrooms.

6. When playing **Judicial Jargon**, have a championship round. Excuse the winning team from the vocabulary list.

Overview of Activities *(cont.)*

Extending the Unit

1. Take a class field trip to observe a real trial (one that would be appropriate for students). Have the students write a paper about what they learned.

2. Research crime statistics. Help students create mathematical problems based on those statistics.

3. Select a mystery play and let students perform the play.

4. Invite someone in the legal profession to be a guest speaker.

5. Have students research some local outdated laws. Discuss how laws change as communities change.

6. If your school has a debate team, ask the advisor and some of the debaters to come to your class and speak about debating issues.

7. Have students watch a debate and encourage them to discuss the results.

8. Set up an informal panel discussion over current topics.

9. Put a list of current topics in a box. Let each student draw a topic and speak for one minute on that topic.

10. Discuss school laws and additions or changes the class would like to see enforced. Write proposals to the student council.

11. Research the legal system used in different countries. Present these reports to the class and have the class discuss the differences.

12. Get day-old copies of the newspaper from your school library. Clip out articles about interesting cases. Have students read the articles and list the evidence presented in each case. From the evidence given, have them decide whether the accused is guilty or innocent.

13. Create your own mystery dinner. Provide students with a simple script. Allow them to dress up as characters and bring food for the event. Read the play as a group and let them guess which one of the characters committed the crime.

14. Plan a school-wide "Kids and the Law" day. Invite guest speakers, parents, and members of the community.

Setting Up Centers

To enhance students' learning, try setting up centers in your classroom. For this particular unit, a variety of interesting materials exist and a variety of ways to use them. Choose or modify any of the activities for your classroom.

Ways of Using Centers

1. **Whole Class Activity**—Divide the class into groups. Give each group a set number of minutes at each center and rotate so that each group gets to use each center.

   Hint: Be careful in balancing your materials so that all the exercises take about the same amount of time. Also, work out some system before you begin that incorporates those who are absent or who need extra time to finish. For example, make up take-home packets before the unit begins.

2. **Enrichment**—Use centers to add to the established activities already in the unit. These centers may include activities such as computer skills, reading comprehension, logic, and writing skills.

3. **Reward**—Use the centers as a break from routine work and a reward for high scores on tests or quizzes, good behavior, winning class review games, improving work, or accomplishing personal goals. Give the student a coupon that may be cashed in at certain times.

4. **Remediation**—Use the centers for remediation. For example, if a student is weak in logic, allow him to go to the computer center and figure out a mystery by using logic and reasoning.

How to Set Up Centers

1. Look at the layout of your room. Try to find space in the back or on the sides to set up small tables or extra desks.

2. Based on space and activities, decide how many centers you need. If you are doing a whole-class activity at centers and you have 25 students, you may want to set up five centers. If you are using centers for remediation, reward, or enrichment, you may need fewer centers.

3. Number and name each center. For example, *Center #1: Logic, Center #2: Reading.* Display the numbers and names so that they will be easily visible to students.

4. Look at your roll and put students in groups.

5. Put an assignment folder at each center. Also, have a place on your desk or at a central spot in the room where students turn in their work when they change centers.

6. Make sure all the materials the students need are at each center.

7. If you choose the whole-class activity, you may want to bring a "minute minder" to class. Inform the students that when they hear the bell, they change centers.

Setting Up Centers *(cont.)*

Suggested Centers for Our Legal System

— Center #1: *Technology* —

Materials:

- Computer(s)
- Printer(s)
- Computer paper
- Computer software
  Suggested Computer Software for this Unit: (See bibliography, page 79.)
  - *In The First Degree* (Other mystery software is available but should be carefully screened.)
  - *Where in the USA Is Carmen Sandiego?*
  - *Do-It-Yourself-Lawyer*

Assignments: Try to solve the mysteries. Write your answers on your paper or generate a computer printout. Let the students print out real legal documents.

Objective: to use logic and reasoning in solving a mystery

— Center #2: *Reading* —

Materials:

- Cushions, bean bag chairs, or comfortable chairs (if possible)
- Reading material
  Suggested Reading Material for this Unit: (See bibliography, page 79.)
  - *Famous Trials* by Frank McLynn
  - A selection of mysteries from the school library
  - Current newspapers

Assignment: Select a reading assignment. Write a summary of your reading.

Objective: to increase reading comprehension

— Center #3: *Writing Center* —

Materials:

- Computer(s)
- Printer(s)
- Computer Paper
- Creative Writing Assignment Sheet (See page 71.)
- Software: Word Processing Program

Assignment: Select a topic and write a paper, using correct punctuation, spelling, and grammar.

Objectives: to improve writing skills, grammar, punctuation, and spelling

Setting Up Centers *(cont.)*

Suggested Centers for Our Legal System *(cont.)*

Center #4: *Graphics*

Materials:

- Computer(s)
- Printer(s)
- Computer paper
- Software: 3-D Furniture (See bibliography, page 79.)
- Crayons and markers
- Paper
- Stencils and rules

Assignment: Create a mystery picture. A crime has been committed in the room that the student creates. Something in the room must be a clue to solve the mystery. Design your office.

Objectives: to improve skills in logic and critical thinking and improve creative thinking skills.

Center #5: *Research Center*

Materials:

- Research materials
- On-line computer
- Printer(s)
- Computer(s)
- List of Research Topics (See pages 40 and 71)
- Suggestions for research materials for this unit: (See lists on pages 6 and 79.)

Assignment: Research a topic and write a short report.

Objectives: to improve research skills and to improve writing skills

Center #6: *Bill of Rights*

Materials:

- Copy of the U.S. Constitution and reference books
- On-line computer
- Printer(s)
- Poster materials

Assignment: Study the first ten amendments to the U.S. Constitution, which became effective on December 15, 1797. Prepare a restatement of each amendment in today's language. Note at least one application or concern today for each amendment, such as gun control, religion in schools, freedom of speech, etc. Prepare a poster to mount in the room for Bill of Rights Day on December 15.

Objectives: to strengthen language skills, reasoning skills, and understanding of our fundamental laws concerning liberty.

U.S. Legal System Chart

The United States has 50 state court systems and one federal court system. No two state courts are run in exactly the same way. Nor is the federal court system more important than the state court system.

Use this chart as a reference as you study the unit.

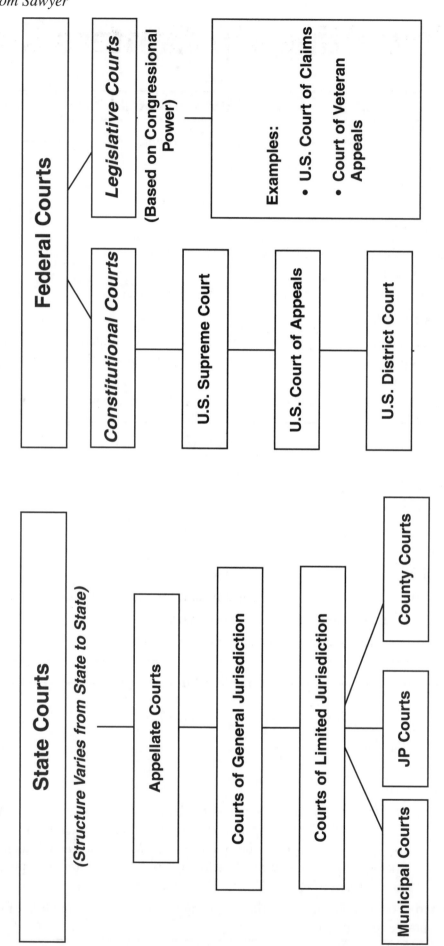

Federal Courts

Legislative Courts

(Based on Congressional Power)

Examples:
• U.S. Court of Claims
• Court of Veteran Appeals

Constitutional Courts

U.S. Supreme Court

U.S. Court of Appeals

U.S. District Court

State Courts

(Structure Varies from State to State)

Appellate Courts

Courts of General Jurisdiction

Courts of Limited Jurisdiction

Municipal Courts

JP Courts

County Courts

12

How the Legal System Works

Our legal system is divided into **state** and **federal** courts. The federal courts are different from the state courts, and each one of the state courts is very different from the other. Each state determines what is socially acceptable behavior and reasonable punishment. Even the structure of each of the state courts is different. In one state, for example, one of their courts may be called a *district court*, while in another state the same type of court is called a *superior court*.

Within the federal system, there are two types of courts: **legislative** and **constitutional**. The Supreme Court is a constitutional court because it rules on matters concerning the Constitution. The lesser constitutional courts were established under Article III of the Constitution which allows Congress to set up constitutional courts inferior to the Supreme Court. Judges in both the Supreme Court and the inferior constitutional courts have lifetime appointments unless their behavior warrants removal. In such a case, the justice would go through an impeachment process before being dismissed.

Legislative courts are established based on Congress' legislative powers. For example, one of the powers Congress has is to organize, arm, and discipline the military. A court was, therefore, created by Congress to discipline soldiers. Unlike the constitutional courts, judges in the legislative courts are not appointed for life.

The federal constitutional courts are organized in three levels.

1. **U.S. District Courts**—Originally, one district court existed in each state. Some states, however, needed more courts than others. Now, 89 courts exist in 50 states. These courts try both criminal and civil cases. One judge presides over the case and a jury hears the evidence. Federal courts are not superior to state courts. The decision of a state court stands unless the case involves a constitutional issue.

2. **U.S. Court of Appeals**—The United States is divided into circuits. One court of appeals hears all the cases for that circuit. Presently, 13 permanent and one temporary U.S. Court of Appeals exists. The courts hear cases on appeal from the U.S. District Courts. Usually, cases in these courts are heard by a panel of three judges. The decision does not have to be unanimous but goes to the majority vote. On some occasions, all the judges assigned to a particular circuit decide to hear the case.

3. **U.S. Supreme Court**—Very few cases ever reach the Supreme Court. Although the Supreme Court receives between 4,000 and 5,000 requests for appeal each year, the court hears only 150 cases per year. Nine justices sit on the Supreme Court—eight associate justices and one Chief Justice. These justices hear the appeals and write decisions based on their interpretation of the Constitution.

How the Legal System Works *(cont.)*

The federal legislative courts are established based on certain areas of responsibility assigned to Congress.

The following are two examples of these courts:

- **U.S. Court of Claims**—This court tries claims against the government involving violation of public contracts.
- **U.S. Court of Veteran Appeals**—This court hears appeals from veterans of military service.

Although the structure of state courts varies from one state to another, most states have courts that in some way correspond to these:

1. **Courts of Limited Jurisdiction**—These courts hear cases of a specialized nature. Examples of these courts are the following:

- *Municipal Courts*—Sometimes called "traffic courts," these courts usually deal with minor offenses and misdemeanors.

- *JP Courts*—Justice of the Peace Courts often perform tasks such as marrying couples, investigating questionable deaths, and preparing the court's yearly budget, which have little to do with judicial responsibilities. However, both criminal and civil cases can be tried in these courts. Usually, the cases are within the limits of certain geographical boundaries and involve misdemeanor offenses limited to small fines and jail sentences. JP courts are often called *small claims courts*.

- *County Courts*—These courts' jurisdictions are limited to county lines. Unlike the other two courts, these courts often try cases in which the fine or jail sentence is relatively high. Appeal from lower courts may also be tried in these courts.

2. **Courts of General Jurisdiction**—These are the major courts of the state. They try both criminal and civil cases, and they try felony offenses.

3. **Appellate Courts**—These courts are usually divided into two levels. The first level allows everyone to have one chance to appeal the decision without going to the *court of last resort*. The court of last resort, sometimes called the State Supreme Court, is usually the last chance for a decision to be reversed, except in rare cases when the case is heard by the U.S. Supreme Court.

Activity: Make a large copy of the U.S. Legal System Chart. Put it on the bulletin board or the classroom wall. Trace the blocks of the smaller chart. Try to fill in the blocks without looking at the original chart.

Enrichment: Our forefathers set up our government to be a system of checks and balances. Explain what you think a system of checks and balances is. How would the court system be an example of a system of checks and balances? Your teacher may ask you to discuss your answer.

Basic Legal Terms

1. **Affidavit**—a sworn statement under oath

2. **Alibi**—an excuse used by the accused which places him or her somewhere else during the crime

3. **Appeal**—a request that a case be retried in a higher court

4. **Argument**—a summary of the case which tries to convince the judge or jury that the person being tried is guilty or innocent

5. **Bail**—security given for the temporary release of a person from jail

6. **Bar Association**—a society of members of the legal profession

7. **Breaking a Case**—solving a case

8. **Case**—a disagreement of the law which is settled in a court of law

9. **Chamber**—a special room or office

10. **Civil Action**—action brought to protect private rights

11. **Confession**—an admission of guilt

12. **Contempt of Court**—an act disrupting legal hearings or challenging the authority of the court

13. **Conviction**—the result of a criminal trial when the accused is found guilty

14. **Court**—a legal assembly to hear the facts of a case

15. **Crime**—an act of breaking the law

16. **Criminal**—one who breaks the law

17. **Criminal Action**—the process of charging, trying, and sentencing the accused of a crime

18. **Decision**—report of the judge's and jury's conclusion of the case

19. **Evidence**—proof concerning the case which is presented at the trial

20. **Examination**—a search for truth which involves asking questions during a trial

Basic Legal Terms *(cont.)*

21. **Fine**—a sum of money the defendant is ordered to pay for wrongdoing

22. **Fugitive**—one who is accused of or has committed a crime and tries to escape the law

23. **Negligence**—failure to take proper precautions resulting in some harm to people or property

24. **Objection**—a statement declaring that evidence entered in a case has been done incorrectly

25. **Parole**—early supervised release of a prisoner

26. **Perjury**—a lie when a promise (a sworn oath) has been made to tell the truth

27. **Plea**—the defendant's response to being accused of a crime

28. **Plea Bargaining**—in a criminal case, an agreement made between the accused and prosecutor to lessen a sentence or avoid a trial

29. **Search Warrant**—a legal document that allows the search and seizure of property

30. **Self-defense**—the right to protect one's body or property against harm

31. **Sentence**—the punishment for a person who has been found guilty of a crime

32. **Subpoena**—a document requiring the appearance of a witness in court

33. **Surveillance**—deliberate observation of people or places associated with a crime

34. **Suspect**—a person who is thought by police to be involved in a crime

35. **Sustain**—to approve an attorney's motion (a judge's action)

36. **Testimony**—a statement made by a witness under oath

37. **Trial**—legal examination of the facts of a case before a judge and possibly a jury

38. **Unconstitutional**—conflicting with the rights guaranteed to every citizen by the Constitution or with any other provision of the U.S. Constitution

39. **Verdict**—conclusion of the jury after they have heard the evidence presented during the trial

40. **Warrant**—a legal document giving authority to do something

Searching for Terms

Fill in the blanks with legal terms. Then find the terms in the puzzle.

```
V  E  R  D  I  C  T  E  S  T  I  M  O  N  Y  S
L  Y  R  U  J  R  E  P  U  E  N  P  E  S  E  E
A  L  A  W  E  E  R  S  S  S  E  L  X  E  L  A
N  C  A  E  S  S  A  Z  P  T  G  E  A  L  L  R
O  F  U  G  I  T  I  V  E  N  L  A  F  F  O  C
I  O  U  W  P  A  R  O  C  O  I  B  I  D  P  H
T  R  I  A  L  T  O  Q  T  I  Q  A  N  E  G  W
U  P  A  R  O  L  E  A  R  T  E  R  E  F  R  A
T  W  E  R  R  A  U  S  T  C  M  G  T  E  S  R
I  S  U  A  R  T  S  A  R  E  C  A  I  N  T  R
T  R  A  N  T  H  P  A  F  J  E  I  O  S  U  A
S  E  N  T  E  N  C  E  K  B  I  N  N  E  V  N
N  S  U  S  T  A  I  N  B  O  I  O  D  W  T  T
O  O  D  D  S  U  B  P  O  E  N  A  Z  X  F  C
C  E  I  W  I  W  S  F  R  E  A  G  L  Q  Y  H
N  E  G  L  I  G  E  N  C  E  A  P  A  E  L  P
U  E  C  N  A  L  L  I  E  V  R  U  S  I  Z  J
```

Clues

1. An agreement made by prosecutor and defendant _____
2. One who escapes the law _____
3. A legal document giving authority _____
4. Decision of the jury _____
5. Not agreeing with the Constitution _____
6. Legal examination of guilt or innocence _____
7. Witness' statement _____
8. To approve _____
9. Observation of people connected to the crime _____
10. Possible criminal _____
11. Document requiring attendance in court _____
12. Punishment for guilty person _____
13. Right to protect self and property _____
14. Carelessness resulting in injury _____
15. Argument against entering evidence in a case _____
16. Early release of prisoner _____
17. Money payment for wrongdoing _____
18. A lie under oath _____
19. Defendant's response to charge _____
20. Document that allows the search of property _____

Judicial Jargon

Judicial Jargon is a review game aimed to help students learn the many new vocabulary words in this unit while they begin to learn basic courtroom procedure. *Level I* helps students with memorization skills, and *Level II* helps students with comprehension skills.

Materials

- Jury Member Cutouts
- Index Cards
- Questions for *Level I* and *Level II*
- Answers for *Level I* and *Level II* (See answer key on page 80 for level II.)

Preparation of Materials

- Run off copies of jury members.
- Cut out jury members.
- Run off copies of questions.
- Cut out questions and paste on the front of index cards.
- Run off copies of answers.
- Paste copies of answers on back of index cards. (You may want to laminate cards for future use.)

Setting Up

1. Introduce students to new vocabulary words in the unit.
2. After students are familiar with the words, divide the class into groups of five.
3. Assign two students to be defense attorneys, two students to be prosecuting attorneys, and one student as a judge. (You may want students to rotate positions as they play.)
4. The judge should be given a box of index cards and a watch with a second hand.

Playing the Game

- ☐ The prosecution and defense teams will compete for points.
- ☐ The judge will control the activities of the game, read the questions, keep time, and award points.
- ☐ The prosecution will begin.
- ☐ The judge will read the first question.
- ☐ The prosecution has 30 seconds to answer correctly.
- ☐ If the prosecution answers incorrectly or goes over the time limit, the question goes to the defense.
- ☐ The defense has 15 seconds to answer correctly.
- ☐ If no one answers the question correctly, the judge reads the answer and continues.
- ☐ If a question is answered correctly, the team is awarded the first of 12 jury members.
- ☐ The first team to collect seven jury members wins the game.
- ☐ If both teams collect six jury members, the game is considered a "mistrial" and a new game must be played.

Judicial Jargon—Level I

——— Definitions and Terms ———

1. Society's rules
2. Person who breaks laws
3. Injury against an individual or his/her property
4. Breaking laws
5. Person accused of a crime
6. Person police think might have done the crime
7. Person who makes a case for or against the defendant
8. Person who defends the accused
9. Person who tries to convict the defendant
10. Person who presides over the trial
11. Order to appear in court
12. What a person says under oath in court
13. Injury against society
14. Person who swears in witnesses
15. Involving the application of science to legal matters
16. Being sentenced to time in prison
17. Being released from prison early for good behavior
18. Person who suffers from the crime
19. Person who examines the dead body in a criminal investigation
20. Questioning by lawyers
21. When a lawyer questions a witness for a second time
22. Lawyer's secretary
23. A request that a case be tried in a higher court
24. Security for temporary release from jail
25. Special office
26. An admission of guilt
27. Proof related to the case
28. One who is accused of a crime and escapes
29. Lying under oath
30. Document allowing for search and seizure of property
31. One who testifies
32. Sworn statement under oath
33. Society of lawyers who deal with ethics of the law
34. Action that disrupts court
35. A deal between prosecution and accused
36. The right to protect one's body
37. Legal action brought to protect private rights
38. Solving a case
39. Report of the judge and jury's conclusion of the case
40. Money paid for wrongdoing

1. Laws
2. Criminal
3. Tort
4. Crime
5. Defendant
6. Suspect
7. Lawyer
8. Defense attorney
9. Prosecuting attorney
10. Judge
11. Subpoena
12. Testimony
13. Crime
14. Bailiff
15. Forensic
16. Incarceration
17. Parole
18. Victim
19. Coroner
20. Examination
21. Cross-examination
22. Legal secretary
23. Appeal
24. Bail
25. Chamber
26. Confession
27. Evidence
28. Fugitive
29. Perjury
30. Search warrant
31. Witness
32. Affidavit
33. Bar Association
34. Contempt of Court
35. Plea Bargaining
36. Self Defense
37. Civil Action
38. Breaking a Case
39. Decision
40. Fine

Judicial Jargon—Level II

1. A lawyer betrayed his client's trust; the client called the group of lawyers concerned with legal ethics named the_____.

2. Linda defended herself against Ralph's attack; the police did not press charges because she has the_____.

3. A prosecutor told Larry that if he would tell him who was selling drugs in the school, he would drop all charges against Larry. This is an example of_____.

4. Mr. Johnson didn't fix his roof, even though he knew it was dangerous. When it caved in during the snowstorm and injured several customers, he was accused of_____.

5. After two years of working on the case, the detective found the missing clue and_____.

6. The police thought that Candy committed the crime. She was their prime _____.

7. Candy hired the best_____in town.

8. Hair, blood samples, and fingerprints were all key_____in the case.

9. Mrs. Rowland's next-door neighbor saw the robbery and became a_____for the defense.

10. _____Sanders ran an orderly courtroom.

11. He left the country before the trial; he was a_____from the law.

12. The lawyer conducted a lengthy_____of the witness.

13. The_____in the trial couldn't decide on a verdict.

14. The prisoner was let out on_____after only six months in jail.

15. When the police came to the door, they had a_____and were able to seize evidence.

16. The judge's_____for the defendant was two years in prison.

17. The_____of the celebrity lasted for almost a year.

18. The defense attorney made an_____to the prosecutor's line of questioning.

19. The_____of the jury was read by the judge.

20. The witness testified that he was at home during the crime; later his claims were proved false, and he was charged with_____.

21. After escorting the prisoners into the room, the_____unlocked their handcuffs.

22. Dismissing the case, the judge retired to his_____.

23. A picture of the_____'s body was shown to the jury.

24. Matt did not want to appear in court; however, he was served with a_____.

25. Jim Thomas, a_____, worked hard to prove the defendant guilty.

26. Mandy was going 55 miles per hour in a 35 miles per hour speed zone. Consequently, she had to pay a large_____.

27. He never dreamed that he would be_____and go to jail.

28. The_____carefully examined the victim's body, deciding that the victim had been poisoned.

29. After the defense attorney examined the witness, the prosecuting attorney asked more questions,_____the witness.

Judicial Jargon *(cont.)*

Jury Members

Run off copies. Cut out and laminate jury members.

Using Your Terms

Directions: Fill in the blanks with your legal terms on pages 15 and 16.

1. The people arrested Tom for the murder, but he had a(n)_____placing him somewhere else during the time of the crime.

2. The judge stayed in his_____until time for the trial.

3. The prosecuting attorney's_____of the witness lasted for two hours.

4. When Jack was arrested, his best friend posted_____for Jack's temporary release from jail.

5. The case was dismissed because the prosecuting attorney did not have enough _____to prove that the defendant was guilty.

6. The_____of the jury was announced after they deliberated for four hours.

7. After the trial, the lawyer who did not agree with the jury's decision filed an_____.

8. The_____of one of the leading members of Congress was a surprise to everyone who thought he would never commit a crime.

9. At noon, the_____was still in session.

10. The attorney made a strong_____for the defendant.

11. After Sarah was apprehended by the police, she made a full_____of the murder.

12. The defendant was charged with_____when he argued with the judge, disrupting the court.

13. When Jerri committed the robbery, she committed a_____.

14. Since she committed a crime, she was considered a_____.

15. She was subject to the process of charging, trying, and sentencing a person accused of a crime called_____.

16. The group of legal professionals called the_____is concerned with the ethics in the legal system.

17. After just a day of investigation, the detective said that_____was simple.

18. The_____of *Brown vs. Simmons* was scheduled to be tried in court on Wednesday.

19. The witness signed a(n)_____that his statement was true.

20. _____was brought against the defendant by the family of the deceased.

History of English Laws

At different times in history, people have had few or no rules. No strong government existed—no laws, prisons, or policemen. In England this time is called the *Dark Ages*. Prior to that, the Roman Empire ruled England. When Rome withdrew its legions in the early 400s, no one was left to enforce laws. Life became nasty, brutal, and violent. Eventually, people began to demand that order be established and laws be enforced. Finally, around 600 A.D., a set of laws was established by Aethelbert, Christian King of Kent. Much later, King Canute, who ruled from 1017 to 1035, added to those rules, restoring and enforcing Anglo-Saxon customs. By the twelfth century, England had an organized system of law and order.

This system was much different from the one today. No lawyers were used, and the facts of a case were not necessarily important. One citizen would make a complaint against another in the form of an oath. The one accused of the crime would respond with a denial and produce witnesses to testify to his character.

In serious cases, 12 citizens would go before the court accusing the defendant. Then, the defendant could be tried in two ways. The first was as in lesser crimes—*to produce people to testify about his or her character*. The second way was called *trial by ordeal*, and several methods were popular. In the first method, the defendant was burned on the hand or arm. If after a few days the wound was clean, the defendant was considered innocent. If the wound was infected, the defendant was declared guilty. The second method was to bind the defendant and throw that person into the water. If the defendant sank, he or she was innocent. If the defendant floated, he or she was guilty. Finally, *trial by combat* resolved conflicts. The two parties fought (or in some cases hired others to fight for them) to determine who was right.

During the reign of Henry II, crimes were wrongdoings against the king as well as the individual. For serious crimes, the king had a council that tried the accused and used juries.

By the end of the thirteenth century, Henry's court had evolved into three courts: *The Court of Common Pleas* for civil disputes; *The Court of the King's Bench* for criminal cases; and *The Court of the Exchequer*, dealing with taxes and money. These courts were all common law courts—that is, courts enforcing laws common to all Englishmen.

Common law court usually required the guilty party to pay damages. Soon, Englishmen realized that they needed another kind of court—one that would keep certain acts from happening. Therefore, the courts of equity were created to issue injunctions—court orders meant to keep a person from doing something harmful.

For 400 years this system of courts remained in England until the common law court and the court of equity were eventually combined, to establish the modern court system of today.

History of American Legal System

Everyone in your classroom is different. Each person comes from a different background with different ideals. What do you think would happen if each student in the classroom described a perfect school? Do you think everyone would agree? Probably not. In the next 10 minutes, write down your description of the perfect school. Now, your teacher will put you in a group of three or four. Answer the following questions as a group. Everyone in the group must agree before you write down your answers.

---

1. What are the five most important classes offered in a school?

2. How many students should be in a school?

3. List the three most important extracurricular activities offered in a school.

4. How many students should be in a classroom?

5. What should be the hours of the school day?

Did your group have trouble deciding on the answers?

If your group had trouble deciding on the description of the perfect school, they were very much like the first settlers who had difficulty deciding on a perfect legal system for their new country. Just like the people in your classroom, everyone came from different backgrounds. Many settlers came from Spain, England, France, and even Holland. Each country had its own set of rules and ways of enforcing them.

The English legal system became the most popular model, but even it did not fit the needs of the colonists. Consequently, the colonists took the English system and made changes. They simplified the court system and emphasized individual rights, religious freedom, and self-sufficiency. Each colony developed new ways of handling conflicts within its own territory. After the Revolutionary War, even more changes were made. For example, before the Revolutionary War, judges were the primary law makers. After the war, however, legislatures representing the voice of the people became the primary law makers.

Group Scenario

Imagine your group is the first to settle a new planet. This planet is named *Zota*. It has been discovered in a galaxy many light years away from Earth. This planet is very much like Earth in that it has plants, animals, oxygen, gravity, and water. Your group is being sent to Zota to live for 10 years. During that time, you are to explore the planet, gather data, and set up a system of laws and ways to enforce these laws.

Your group votes to begin with five important laws. Discuss what are the most important laws for your society and how you plan to enforce these laws. You may be asked to share your answers.

Breaking the Law

When someone breaks the law, a *tort* or a *crime* is committed. The word *tort* comes from the Latin word meaning *twisted*. When someone commits a tort, that person damages another person or that person's property. Usually the person committing the tort is required to pay money to the injured person.

A *crime* occurs when someone breaks a law that hurts society. When someone commits a crime, usually that person serves time in prison.

Five of the following situations are crimes. The rest are torts. Try to decide which are the crimes and which are the torts. Write the numbers of the crimes on your paper and explain why you selected those answers. Your teacher may ask you to discuss your answers.

1. The police received a call that a murder had been committed.

2. A minor traffic incident occurred at the corner of Vine Street and Cherry Avenue. Mr. James dented Mr. Johnson's fender.

3. A fisherman has been fishing in the Jones' pond without permission.

4. A tourist destroyed a painting in the local art gallery.

5. James threatened the teacher when she didn't give him an A in math.

6. Mr. Donner didn't like his landlord, so he set fire to his apartment building.

7. The local bank was robbed this morning.

8. Chad had been the quarterback his junior year. Tom was a new student with more athletic ability than Chad. When the coaches replaced Chad with Tom, Chad gave Tom a black eye.

9. At the mall, a small child wandered away from her mother and was kidnapped.

10. In Pinewood Estates, the police got complaints that a man was spying on his neighbors with a telescope.

Activity: Look through the newspaper. Cut out two articles—one illustrating a tort and the other a crime. Explain the differences between the two. Post your articles and explanation on the bulletin board or make transparencies to show the class on an overhead projector.

Kids and Laws

Did you know that even though you are not an adult, you are still expected to follow the laws? Breaking a law is considered to be a tort or crime. When crimes are committed by kids, they have to go to court, too. Usually, kids are not tried in adult courts. Instead, they are tried in juvenile court, a special court for children up to the age of 18.

Listed for you are crimes that kids might commit.

Without looking up these words, write down what you believe the definition of each of these crimes is. Then, look up the words and see how many of them you got right.

Arson _____

Vandalism _____

Conversion _____

Larceny _____

Burglary _____

Robbery _____

Read each of the following situations. Write down the name of the crime you believe is about to be committed.

Situations

1. The local middle school has a really good football team. This season has been the best one in 10 years! All the fans are really excited and want to support the team, especially for the big game this weekend. The colors of the school are red and black. A group of students from the middle school decides to go over to the rival school and spray-paint the school's statue of their mascot red and black. _____

2. All the boys in the neighborhood plan to rollerblade in the park this afternoon. Sam doesn't have any rollerblades, but he knows his next door neighbor does. He also knows his neighbor and his family will not be home until 10:00 tonight. Sam doesn't have permission to use the skates, but he decides to borrow them anyway._____

3. Jane lost her science book. She knows her mother will be upset if she has to pay for it, so she decides to open another person's locker and take a book to replace hers. _____

4. Everyone knows that Billy is the bully of the school. He is bigger than the other kids. Every morning waiting for the bus, he beats up on one of the smaller kids in his neighborhood and takes his lunch money. _____

5. The band director told Jake that he could not march this weekend because he had a bad attitude. To get revenge, Jake decided to set the band bus on fire. _____

6. LouAnn has to pass the final exam to pass Miss Taylor's English class. She knows where Miss Taylor keeps the answer keys. She decides to break into Miss Taylor's filing cabinet at lunch.

Types of Crimes and Punishments

In your home and school, are some rules more important than other rules? What happens when you break these rules? Are the consequences the same for talking in class and for fighting? Why do you believe they are different? Just as some rules in the home and school are more important than others, some laws in the community and nation are more important than others.

- The most serious crimes are called *felonies*.
- Less serious crimes are called *misdemeanors*, not as serious as felonies.
- The least serious crimes are called *infractions*.

Just as there are different types of crimes, there are different types of punishments.

1. **Probation**—The defendant is allowed to stay in the community but must check in with a probation officer and follow strict rules.
2. **Suspended Sentence**—The defendant is given a punishment, but the judge decides that person does not have to serve that sentence if he or she participates in a community program of some type.
3. **Parole**—As a result of good behavior, the defendant does not have to serve a full sentence.
4. **Capital Punishment**—The defendant pays for the crime through the loss of his or her life.
5. **Fine**—The defendant is asked to pay money to the court.
6. **Incarceration**—The defendant serves a prison sentence.

How do the crimes and punishments match?

Misdemeanors usually result in serving time at the city or county correctional facilities.

Felonies usually result in a prison sentence at the state penitentiary or the federal penitentiary.

Unscramble the Crime

Mr. Jones' neighbors described him as a sweet, older man whom they never suspected of being a jewel thief. However, they did wonder where he got all his money. He was always traveling to exotic places, claiming he flew on his son's frequent flier miles. Still, his neighbors were shocked when he was arrested for smuggling very small but very valuable rubies into the country. They were even more shocked when they discovered where he had hidden the jewels.

After you unscramble the words below, you will find where he hid the rubies by reading the words spelled by the circled letters.

1. neif ◯ _ _ _
2. noiatborp _ _ _ ◯ _ _ _ _
3. elapor _ _ _ _◯_
4. seinolfe _ _ _ _ _ _ _◯
5. conernovis _ _ _ _◯_ _ _ _ _
6. frincasinot _ _ _ _ _ _◯_ _ _ _
7. rsonaemesdim _ _ _ _ _◯_ _ _ _ _ _
8. cmrise _ _ _ _◯_
9. iiaannccrreot _ _ _ _ _ _ _ _◯_ _ _
10. latipac shinemntup _ _ _ _ _ _ _   _ _ _ _◯_ _ _ _

Evidence

Evidence is information about a crime which is used to prove a defendant guilty or innocent. The three forms of evidence are as follows:

1. *Tangible Evidence*—Physical exhibits
2. *Judicial Notice*—Facts that are found in credible reference books
3. *Oral Testimony*—Testimony by a witness

Tangible evidence is divided into two groups: real evidence and demonstrative evidence.

- *Real evidence* is evidence that can be touched.

   Examples: *a gun, knife, piece of clothing*

- *Demonstrative evidence* is evidence in the form of visual or auditory aids.

   Examples: *charts, graphs, tapes*

Judicial notice is evidence in the form of facts that are generally known or accepted or that can be proved through use of a reference book.

   Example: *Florida has a tropical climate.*

Oral testimony is the most common form of evidence. Oral testimony is given by witnesses who are sworn to tell the truth. If they lie on the witness stand, they commit perjury and may go to jail. Witnesses may tell about what they observed, what they know about the character of the defendant, or what they know about a specific subject. Witnesses who are called to testify about a specific subject are called *expert witnesses.*

   Examples: *A psychologist may testify about the personality of the defendant. A police officer may testify about what he or she found at the scene of the crime.*

Hint: If students write a trial, they need to use this page as a guide when including evidence in their cases.

History of Fingerprints

Do you have an interest in *dactyloscopy?* Mark Twain did. In his book, *Life on the Mississippi,* Twain became the first author to mention the study of fingerprinting. Before fingerprinting became an acceptable way of catching criminals, Mark Twain apprehends the murderer in his novel through fingerprint identification.

Fingerprinting was not an accepted means of finding criminals until the late 1800s. In 1897 the Indian government replaced *anthropometry* (measurement of the human body and its proportions) with *dactyloscopy.* Shortly thereafter in 1901, fingerprinting became a popular method of apprehending criminals at London's Scotland Yard. Fingerprinting was used as early as 618 in China when a husband was required to put his thumbprints on divorce papers. However, only through the hard work of William James Herschel, Sir Francis Galton, Dr. Henry Faulds, Edward Henry, and Juan Vuchtrich was fingerprinting finally accepted as a method of identifying criminals.

William James Herschel used fingerprints on documents to emphasize the importance of business contracts. Throughout the years, he collected thousands of fingerprints, noticing that no two fingerprints were exactly alike. He also observed that fingerprints did not appear to change with age. When he tried to share his discovery with the inspector general of a prison in India, the inspector general was not interested in Herschel's findings.

At about the same time, Dr. Henry Faulds was studying prehistoric pottery in Tokyo, Japan. He also began collecting prints, observing that none of them were the same. In 1880 he published his discoveries in a British magazine called *Nature,* and in 1886 offered to set up a fingerprinting system for Scotland Yard. However, Scotland Yard did not begin using fingerprinting as a supplement to the anthropometric system of detection until 1893, after the publication of Sir Francis Galton's book, *Fingerprints.* In this work, Galton used some of Herschel's data, as well as his own, and devised a system for using fingerprinting as a means of detection.

Edward Henry was the one who simplified the system of fingerprinting, discovering five basic patterns for prints: *arches, tented arches, radial loops, ulnar loops*, and *whorls*. He assigned letters to each pattern, enabling any investigators studying the same print to come up with the same code.

Finally, an Argentine detective named Juan Vucetrich put the method of fingerprinting to the true test. He took a system that he had been developing to check a bloody fingerprint on a piece of wood. The fingerprint led to the startling confession of a murderer who had killed her two sons and then inflicted wounds on herself.

Activity: Look at your own fingerprints.

Materials: shiny metal object, powder, flashlight

Procedure: Grasp the metal object with your fingers. Dust the object with powder. Blow off excess powder. Shine a flashlight on the object. Your prints should be visible.

Drawing of the Crime Scene

Your teacher will set up a crime scene for you. On the sheet provided, make a detailed drawing of the crime scene. Make sure you draw the setting to scale.

Crime Scene Checklist

When you arrive at the crime scene, here is a checklist to help you with your investigation. Of course, this is a very short list compared to a real investigation, but it will give you a good idea of what needs to be done and alert you to the basic steps in a criminal investigation. For more information, you may want to research criminal investigations or invite a police detective to share information with your class.

1. **Secure the area.**

   Write down names and addresses of possible witnesses at the scene. Examine the area but do not disturb the evidence. Mark off the area to show that it is a police investigation.

2. **Take photographs of the crime scene.**

   Before the evidence is disturbed, take pictures of the crime scene. Take a variety of pictures from different angles in the room.

3. **Begin examining the evidence. Make notes as you investigate.**

   Much of the evidence will be examined in the laboratories, but dust for fingerprints, notice patterns of blood drops, ask witnesses questions, and prepare DNA and soil samples.

4. **Try to determine the time and cause of death.**

5. **Begin compiling a profile of the criminal.**

6. **Read and examine any written communication found at the crime scene. Listen to any recorded oral communication—such as answering machines.**

7. **Write a report concerning your findings.**

Investigation

A crime has been committed. What happens next? This is a chart of all that happens. Use this chart in the simulation of the investigation. Each student plays a part and has a job to do, including the body! Remember that the evidence is hidden, so you have to look closely for clues.

☐ **Discovery**

Discover the body.

☐ **Notification**

Someone calls the police.

☐ **Dispatch**

A dispatcher receives the call and notifies the police.

☐ **Police Control of Scene**

The police make sure that witnesses are identified and that none of the evidence is disturbed.

☐ **Detectives Search for Clues**

(See Crime Scene Checklist, page 31.)

☐ **Crime Scene Division Collection of Physical Evidence**

A sketch of the body and surroundings is drawn; photographs are taken; blood, hair, DNA samples are taken; and the presence of fingerprints is established.

☐ **EMT** (Emergency Medical Technicians)

Examine and transport the body.

☐ **Coroner**

Examines body for clues.

☐ **K-9 Unit**

Tracks criminal.

☐ **Secretary**

Types reports of officers and detectives.

☐ **Crime Laboratory Technicians**

Perform tests on evidence.

☐ **Records**

All data are recorded and forms are filled out.

☐ **District Attorney**

Presents case in court.

Investigator's Report

Location:

Name:

Investigation:

Statements:

Scene Description:

Evidence:

Motive, Means, and Opportunity

After the evidence is collected, investigators try to find suspects. Suspects are people who may have committed the crime. In order to accuse someone of a crime, the investigator must prove that the person had motive, means, and opportunity to commit the crime.

1. **Motive:** a reason to want to commit the crime

2. **Means:** the ability to commit the crime

3. **Opportunity:** a chance to have committed the crime

Read the case files of Fairy Tales Investigator, Cindy Rella. See if you can help establish motive, means, and opportunity for her suspects.

Case #1: The Case of the Missing Grandmother

Friday at 5:00 p.m., Cindy gets a call from 501 Little Red Riding Hood Lane. The caller is a young girl who claims that a Mr. Horace Wolf has attacked and eaten her grandmother. When Cindy arrives at the scene, she tries to calm the little girl who eventually is able to tell her story. She was on the way to her grandmother's house when Mr. Wolf stopped her and asked her what was in her basket. Knowing that she should not talk to strangers, the child stated that she was frightened and tried to run from Mr. Wolf. When she did, the cloth on her basket flew off, and Mr. Wolf saw the goodies in the basket. He tried to grab the basket, but at that moment a Forest County policeman drove by and Mr. Wolf disappeared. The girl continued to her grandmother's house. When she got there she was surprised that the door was open. Worried about her grandmother, she rushed through the door and into the bedroom. What she found was not her grandmother but Mr. Wolf dressed like her grandmother. At first, she didn't notice because the figure was under the covers, but when Mr. Wolf opened his mouth, she noticed his long teeth. She screamed, and he lunged at her. Fortunately, the next-door neighbor walked in with an armful of wood. Her grandmother had a fireplace, and Mr. Axson would bring over wood once a month. The little girl added that her grandmother was lazy and never chopped her own wood. Seeing Mr. Axson, Mr. Wolf jumped out the back window, taking the glass with him. The little girl said she was surprised at how big and muscular Mr. Wolf was.

Later, Cindy found out that the neighbor was Mr. Wolf's parole officer. Mr. Wolf had a long criminal history involving theft and violence. (The parole officer cited one gruesome event involving three little pigs.)

Cindy also found out that Mr. Wolf lived in the neighborhood. He had probably been watching the little girl and her grandmother for some time.

Finally, Cindy asked the little girl what was in the basket. She explained that her grandmother refused to keep her money in the bank. Every week, she would bring her grandmother her weekly allowance, $50,000.

Motive, Means, and Opportunity *(cont.)*

Case #1: The Case of the Missing Grandmother *(cont.)*

Help Cindy decide on motive, means, and opportunity. On your paper answer the following questions.

1. What was Mr. Wolf's motive in killing the grandmother? What did he want?

2. Did Mr. Wolf have means to kill the grandmother? Was he strong enough? Was there anything about him that would have helped him commit the murder?

3. Did he have an opportunity to commit the murder? Did anyone see him at the scene of the crime?

Case #2: The Case of the Missing Porridge

Cindy was called to 34 Bear Alley at 7:00 P.M. Thursday night. A burglary had occurred. The Bears, a prominent family in the neighborhood, had been on a trip to Honey Grove Mall and returned to find their house in disarray. Three items appeared to be missing: an antique chair, a mahogany bed, and a porcelain bowl filled with oatmeal that had been sitting on the table from breakfast. What Cindy found unusual about the burglary was that the thief had apparently tried the oatmeal left in the other two bowls. Fingerprints were found on both of the spoons. Also, the thief had apparently sat in the other two antique chairs but had only taken one. The smallest chair was broken. Finally, the thief had slept in the other two beds. The covers were out of order and blonde hair was on the pillows.

After looking at the evidence, Cindy knew she had her suspect. She immediately got in her car and headed toward Antique Boutique. When she arrived, she asked to speak to the owner, Gold E. Locks. Miss Locks appeared, and Cindy asked Miss Locks to show her around the store. Miss Locks seemed pleased and explained that she dealt in only the best antiques and collectibles. She personally tested every chair and bed to make sure they were not only beautiful but functional as well.

She seemed surprised when Cindy asked where she had been earlier in the day. Gold stated that she was by herself collecting antiques for her shop. Cindy asked if she knew the Bears. Gold replied that she did. She said they had a lovely house but she thought some of their antique furniture, although beautiful, was not very useful. Cindy asked her how she knew what the inside of the house looked like when she had never had an invitation from the Bears. Gold said that she had never actually been in the house. Several of her customers had described the house to her. Cindy deduced that she had solved her case.

1. Why would Cindy think she had found her burglar?

2. Try to decide what Gold E. Locks' motive, means, and opportunity were for committing the crime.

Suspect Identification Form

When you examine evidence at the crime scene, make sure to ask the witnesses if they saw anyone around the scene of the crime. From their answers, you may be able to identify suspects who may have been involved in the crime.

1. What were the **sex**, the approximate **age**, **height**, and **weight** of the person(s)?

2. Describe the person's **face**, including **nose**, **eyebrows**, **chin**, **lips**, and **mouth**.

3. If the person is a male, did he have any **facial hair**?

4. Did the person have any **unusual marks** on him or her?

5. What type of **clothes** was the person wearing?

6. Do you know anything about that person? Where does he or she work? Have you seen him or her before?

7. Was the person wearing any **jewelry** that you remember?

After you have interrogated all your witnesses, use the space below to sketch your suspect.

Suspect Sketch

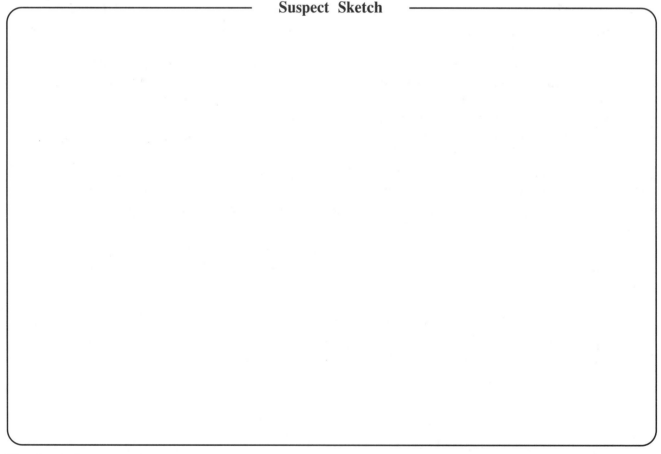

Teacher's Note: During your trial, you may want to give the witnesses clues. The detectives can use the clues to help determine a suspect or suspects for the trial. For an enrichment activity, you may want to plant clues that point to several class members. Then, through interrogation, the detectives or the class can decide who they want to arrest for the crime.

Before the Trial

The Case of Miranda vs. Arizona

In 1963 Ernesto Miranda was tried in an Arizona court. Before the trial, he was cross-examined for two hours with no attorney present. Miranda was coerced into signing a confession which was used in the trial. The United States Supreme Court ruled in 1966 that the procedures used violated Miranda's constitutional rights. Later, however, Miranda was retried and still found guilty.

The Arrest

Before the case of *Miranda vs. Arizona*, police officers did not have to inform suspects of their constitutional rights. Now a case may not be admissible in a court of law if a police officer forgets to read the suspect his or her rights. These rights include the following:

1. *The right to remain silent*

   The suspect does not have to answer questions the police ask.

2. *The right to an attorney, either appointed or retained*

   The suspect has a right to defense. Either the suspect may retain a lawyer or if he or she cannot afford it, a lawyer will be appointed. This lawyer is paid by the government to defend anyone who chooses that service.

3. *The right to know anything he or she says will be used against him or her in a court of law*

   If the suspect chooses to talk to the police, anything he or she says may be used in the case against him or her.

Pretrial Procedures

After a suspect is arrested, many steps occur before that suspect is actually taken to court.

1. The suspect appears before the judge, bond is set, or in some cases bond is denied.

2. The suspect appears at a preliminary hearing. This hearing determines whether enough evidence exists to go to trial. The prosecuting attorney must have established *probable cause*. (Did the suspect have motive, means, and opportunity to commit the crime?) The suspect may waive his rights to a preliminary hearing.

3. If the judge thinks there is enough evidence, the defendant is bound over for trial.

4. Usually, the next step is that a grand jury decides whether the accused should be tried for a crime. The grand jury is a group of 12 to 23 people. If they believe that the suspect should be tried, they pass a true bill, declaring there is enough evidence to warrant a trial. Some states do not use a grand jury. Instead, they use prosecutors to issue an indictment by information.

5. The accused then appears before the judge for an *arraignment*, is formally accused of the charge, and is asked to enter a plea. Before the arraignment, the prosecuting attorney and the accused may work out an agreement in which the accused pleads guilty in exchange for a lesser penalty. If the accused pleads *nolo contendere*, it means he or she pleads no contest to the charges and the judge may go ahead and sentence him or her.

6. If by this point, the accused has not been released, made a plea bargain, or made a plea of *nolo contendere*, he or she is ready to go to trial.

People in the Courtroom

During a trial, many people participate. The people listed below are some of the people you see when court is in session.

- ❑ **Defendant:** The person who is accused of committing the crime
- ❑ **Defense Attorney:** The lawyer who argues the case for the defendant
- ❑ **Prosecuting Attorney:** The lawyer who argues the case for the people
- ❑ **Legal Secretary:** Secretary of a lawyer
- ❑ **Clerk of the Court:** Officer of the court who keeps the records of the trials and court proceedings
- ❑ **Bailiff:** A court officer who is in charge of keeping order, custody of the jury, and custody of the prisoners while court is in session
- ❑ **Judge:** An officer of the court who presides over the trial
- ❑ **Jury:** A group of citizens temporarily selected to listen to the facts of a case and decide whether the defendant is innocent or guilty
- ❑ **Witness:** One who testifies to what he has seen or heard

Directions: Based on the information above, fill in the blanks of the story with the correct terms.

Mrs. Wood received a phone call at 7:30 A.M., Friday morning. She was informed that her son had been arrested for theft. She immediately called their family lawyer, Mr. P. Cook, who was the best (1)_____ in town. She knew her son Sam could not have committed the crime. After hearing Sam's story, Mr. Cook agreed with Mrs. Wood.

On the day of the trial, Mrs. Wood watched as her son, the (2)_____ in the case, was brought into the court by the (3)_____. She looked at the (4)_____, which consisted of four men and eight women. She hoped that they would listen closely to the evidence before making a decision. Next, she looked at the (5)_____, Mr. Charles Crisp. He was known to be a fair but tough lawyer who worked very hard for the people. At the table with Sam and Mr. Cook was Mrs. Phillips, a very competent but overworked (6)_____. This morning Mrs. Phillips looked especially tired. She probably had stayed up late helping prepare Sam's defense. Finally, Mrs. Wood noticed that the (7)_____ in the case was a woman, Mrs. Gilchrist. Mrs. Gilchrist looked very stern sitting on the bench with her black robe. If the jury found her son guilty, Mrs. Wood was afraid Mrs. Gilchrist's sentence would be harsh. During the trial, she watched as the (8)_____ kept record of the trial. She wondered how she could keep up with what everyone said. By 5:00 the trial was over and Mrs. Wood's son was set free. Her lawyer found a (9)_____, Mr. Carter, a prominent businessman, who had seen Sam in Tina's, a local restaurant, at the time of the crime.

Courtroom Cutouts

This is a picture of a courtroom in session; however, the people are missing. After reading a description of the people, place the proper persons in the correct location in the courtroom.

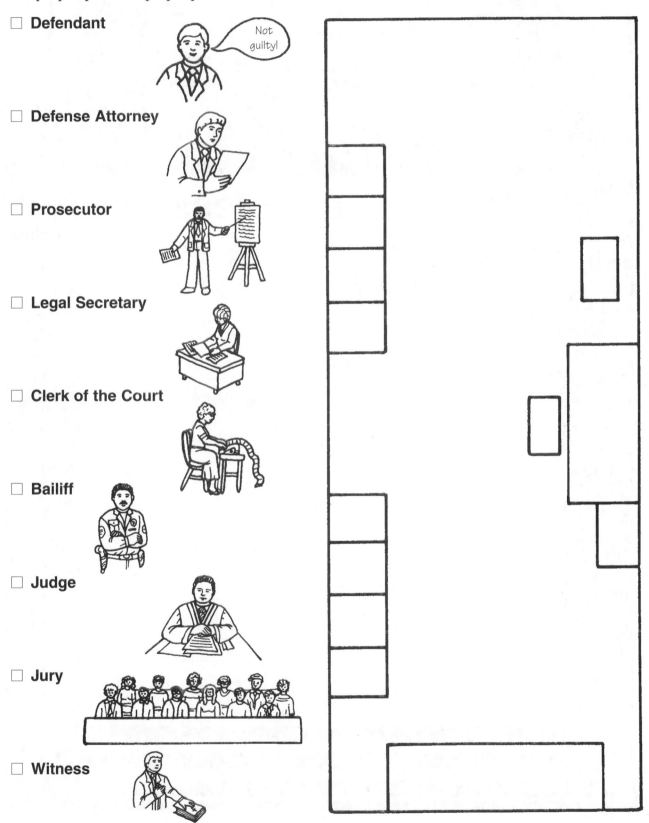

☐ **Defendant**

☐ **Defense Attorney**

☐ **Prosecutor**

☐ **Legal Secretary**

☐ **Clerk of the Court**

☐ **Bailiff**

☐ **Judge**

☐ **Jury**

☐ **Witness**

Research a Profession

- Fingerprint Expert
- Crime Scene Photographer
- Forensic Pathologist
- Forensic Psychologist and Psychiatrist
- Forensic Serologist
- Forensic Dentists and Ondontologist
- Ballistics Expert
- Forensic Chemist
- Forensic Geologist
- Forensic Entomologist
- Forensic Anthropologist
- Forensic Artist

- Forensic Sculptor
- Forensic Linguist
- Police Detective
- Newspaper Reporter
- Prosecuting Attorney
- Defense Attorney
- Judge
- Legal Secretary
- Court Reporter
- Bailiff
- Criminalist
- Detective

Courtroom Procedure Chart

What happens during a trial? Study and use this chart during your mock trial.

❏ **Opening Statement**—*an introduction, usually addressed to the jury*

The opening statement includes an overview of the case and asserts that the accused is guilty or innocent, depending on the prosecution's opening statement or the defense's opening statement. The prosecution begins, followed by the defense.

❏ **Direct Examination**—*interrogation of witnesses sworn to tell the truth*

The lawyers ask the witnesses questions in front of the judge and jury.

❏ **Cross Examination**—*interrogation following direct examination*

After one lawyer asks a witness questions, the opposing lawyer asks the same witness questions.

❏ **Redirect Examination**—*a return to the original interrogating lawyer*

If important information is revealed during the testimony of the witness for the opposing lawyer, the first lawyer may ask permission to ask more questions.

❏ **Recross Examination**—*a return to the cross examination*

The opposing lawyer gets a chance to ask additional questions.

❏ **Closing Statement**—*a summary of the important evidence and arguments in the case*

The prosecution makes his presentation first. This is a lawyer's last chance to persuade the jury.

❏ **Verdict**—*the final decision*

The jury decides whether the accused is guilty or innocent.

Options: The Court Case

Option #1

When students write their own court case, the mock trial is even more fun for them. This lesson plan has proved very successful in the classroom and can be modified for different age and ability levels. It is always a day students look forward to and always a day they talk about later. When you actually have the students write the trial, you must add time to your unit. If you have access to computers, this is a good activity for the word processor.

Hints: Take all the students through the writing process one step at a time. Allow enough time—about a week for students to write the case and a day to put on the trial. Save some time to show the film to the class. (Even though your curriculum is full, think of all the skills and learning objectives you are covering in just one unit!)

Day 1

Make a list of all the evidence that the students have collected.

Make a list of all suspects other than the accused. Make a list of all witnesses. Have each student copy the lists so that everyone will have the same evidence. Have each student decide whether he or she wants to be a prosecuting attorney or a defense attorney.

Day 2

Begin the class by pulling out a prize or prize(s). Tell the student that they have 10 minutes to write why they need the prize more than anyone else in the room. Have them read their responses aloud. Award the prize(s).

Explain to them that they tried to persuade you to pick them. In a murder trial, a defense or prosecuting attorney tries to persuade the jury whether the accused is innocent or guilty. At this point, watching an opening statement helps. Play a tape of one of the old classics such as *Perry Mason* or select an opening statement from a real trial, such as one played on CNN. Discuss the material in an opening statement. Explain that an opening statement needs to address the jury. It needs to give basic reasons why the defendant is innocent or guilty, and it needs to assert that the defendant is innocent or guilty. Allow them time to write their opening statements. Monitor their progress.

Day 3

As students come into the classroom, have a dramatic situation set up for them to observe (a brief, rehearsed quarrel or disagreement between two students over a disputed possession—that type of thing). Don't tell them that the situation is not real. When everyone is seated, ask them to write down what they saw. Then, ask them to share their writings. Even though they witnessed the event, they may have different stories. Relate this exercise to witnesses in a court trial. Ask them to select three witnesses from their witness list. Again, at this point, showing film or witnesses testifying is helpful. Ask them to write questions for the witnesses and their answers.

Options: The Court Case *(cont.)*

Day 4

Tell the students that you are going to play a memory game. Read a list of 20 items. After you have finished, ask them to list those items. When they have finished, read out items again and ask the students to put checks by the ones they got right. Ask them whether they remembered more items at the beginning of the list or at the end of the list. Most will probably say at the end. Ask them what teachers do when they get to the end of a paper. They will probably say, "put a grade on the paper." Then ask them how important they believe the lawyers' last statements to the jury should be. Emphasize that those statements are the last chance the lawyers have to persuade the jury. Again, show an example. Explain that the closing statement is a summary of the most important information presented in the trial. Allow them time to read their closing statements. Let them get in pairs and read their statements to each other and make suggestions.

Day 5

This is a good day to do centers with the rest of the class. Select the best prosecuting attorney's case and the best defense attorney's case. Have them work together while the other students work in centers. The two attorneys combine their cases to make a trial. However, they leave the decision to the jury. After they have combined their cases, parts are assigned to classmates and the date of the trial is set. Each person needs to decide on a costume and needs to be familiar with the script. Since students have limited time, a copy of the script may be given to each lawyer and to the judge. Also, a copy may be placed on the witness stand and in the jury box.

Option #2

If you don't have time for students to write their own trial, you may want to try prewritten trials. One of these options is *Justice and Dissent* (Prentice Hall, 1996). These packets include historical backgrounds of famous trials, individual role sheets for all the members in the court, evidence exhibits, questions, and a bibliography.

Suggestions for the Trial Day

- On the bulletin board, post a diagram of the courtroom showing the character assignments and where each student will sit.

- Pass out the diagram two days before the trial (if a student is absent, he or she will have time to get a copy).

- Make sure every participant is familiar with the script.

- Have students bring or select costumes at the beginning of the week.

- Friday is a good day for the trial.

- Tell students that all will be graded during the trial, whether they are participants or in the audience.

- Have a student who is familiar with video equipment tape the trial.

- Ask a parent to come in and help that day.

- Emphasize that the students will be given a brief amount of time at the beginning of class to set up. They must be ready by that time.

- Arrange the classroom like the diagram before the students enter.

- Have a follow-up activity ready in case the taping ends early.

Tom Sawyer Chapter Activities

Included in these pages are questions and activities related to Mark Twain's *The Adventures of Tom Sawyer*. They may be modified to fit your classroom.

❏ **Chapter 1**

Discussion: What is the setting of the story? Describe Tom. How does he get out of doing work? Use five adjectives to describe Sid.

Activities: Using a shoebox mounted on cardboard, recreate Tom's home and yard.

Using the map of the Mississippi River (page 51), locate where Tom lives.

Research Hannibal, Missouri.

Research facts about the South in the 1800s.

Interview your classmates about times they have tried to get out of doing work.

❏ **Chapter 2**

Discussion: How does Tom get the other boys to paint the fence? Why does he make a profit from the other boys? Do you agree with Twain's observation that "Work consists of whatever a body is obliged to do and that play consists of whatever a body is not obliged to do." Why or why not?

Activities: Come up with your own definition for *work*. Type it on the computer, experimenting with fonts and styles. This is a famous scene from *Tom Sawyer*. As a group project, illustrate the scene on a large piece of butcher paper, or using sidewalk chalk, illustrate different scenes on the sidewalk in front of the school (after getting permission from the principal, of course).

❏ **Chapter 3**

Discussion: Why does Aunt Polly reward Tom? How does Tom get revenge on Sid? Who is Amy Lawrence? Why is Tom upset at dinner?

Activities: Research dialects in different regions. Complete the activity on Southern Dialect (page 66). Look at Southern recipes. Prepare a Southern dish and share it with your classmates.

❏ **Chapter 4**

Discussion: What does Tom hate about going to church? How does Tom get the tickets the children earned for reciting Bible verses? Describe the scene at the Sunday school. How does Tom get the Bible? How does the minister find out Tom cheated? Describe Mary.

Activities: Collect pictures of old Southern churches and display them in the classroom. Listen to old Southern spirituals and discuss the history behind them.

❏ **Chapter 5**

Discussion: Describe two of Twain's characters in the church. How does Twain use humor in the scene with the dog and the beetle? What does Tom regret at the end of the chapter?

Activities: After reading the chapter, list practical jokes you have played or seen played. Interview your parents and ask them if they ever participated in practical jokes as children. Make a list of Tom's good and bad qualities. Share them with your classmates.

Tom Sawyer Chapter Activities *(cont.)*

❏ **Chapter 6**

Discussion: How does Tom attempt to stay home from school? Why do his friends envy him for losing a tooth? How does Twain describe Huckleberry Finn? Why do the boys decide to visit the cemetery? What girls does Tom like?

Activities: Describe a time when you tried to convince your parents you were sick so you could stay home from school. What did you think the tooth fairy looked like when you were young? Have you ever wandered through a cemetery at night? In a paragraph, describe what it was like or what you think it would be like.

❏ **Chapter 7**

Discussion: Why does Tom leave school? In this book, who is Tom's best friend?

Activities: Make a list of qualities a best friend should possess.

Following this pattern, write a short poem about your best friend:

Best friend's first name

Two words to describe that person

Son or daughter of

Who loves to . . .

And hates to . . .

Has been my friend since . . .

Two more words to describe that person

Best friend's last name

Make a photo album of you and your best friend's adventures and put it on display in the classroom. Illustrate the adventures of Tom and his best friend and display it on a poster.

❏ **Chapter 8**

Discussion: Why does Tom believe he has failed? What game do Joe and Tom play?

Activities: Read about the legend of Robin Hood. Make up a board game based on Robin Hood.

❏ **Chapter 9**

Discussion: Where do Tom and Huck go? What do they see?

Activities: Have you ever been somewhere you weren't supposed to be and witnessed something that was against the law? Write a paragraph describing why it might be difficult to report such an incident. After reading the chapter, discuss what you would have done if you had seen what Tom and Huck saw. Read famous epitaphs. Write your own epitaph for a famous person.

Tom Sawyer Chapter Activities *(cont.)*

❏ **Chapter 10**

Discussion: What do the boys decide to do about what they witnessed? Why? How does Aunt Polly find out about Tom's adventure?

Activities: Have you ever promised to keep a secret and then broken the promise? Write a paragraph describing what happened.

❏ **Chapter 11**

Discussion: How does Tom feel about Muff Potter being accused of murder? What does Tom do about it? Describe Muff Potter.

Activities: Begin a time line of the crime and the events associated with it. Make a word scramble with character names from Chapters 1–11.

❏ **Chapter 12**

Discussion: Why is Tom upset at the beginning of Chapter 12? How does Aunt Polly try to cure Tom? What does Tom do with Aunt Polly's cure?

Activities: Research home remedies. Discuss some of the more interesting ones you find with the class. Interview anyone in your community who might use or practice home remedies.

❏ **Chapter 13**

Discussion: As a result of his unhappiness, what does Tom decide to do? Whom does he take with him?

Activities: Think about a time you have wanted to run away. Using art clay, create the perfect place to go. Let it dry for several days and then paint it.

❏ **Chapter 14**

Discussion: Describe the boys' first day. What do the townspeople think? How do the boys know what the townspeople think?

Activities: Imagine that you have run away. Keep a diary of the days you are gone. Research different survival skills. Demonstrate one to the class.

❏ **Chapter 15**

Discussion: Where does Tom go? What upsets him?

Activities: Make a list of Tom's good and bad traits. How has the list changed since the beginning of the book? Listen to your teacher as he or she explains round and flat characters. Write an essay explaining whether Tom is a round or flat character.

Tom Sawyer Chapter Activities *(cont.)*

❑ **Chapter 16**

Discussion: What do Joe and Huck want to do? How does Tom stop them? What do they try?

Activities: Can you remember a time you were homesick? Write a children's story about a little girl or boy who is homesick. Illustrate these stories and donate them to a kindergarten or first grade class.

❑ **Chapter 17**

Discussion: How does Becky feel at the beginning of this chapter? When do the boys return? What is the reaction of the town?

Activities: Write a country song about losing someone or something you love, or write the "Ballad of Tom Sawyer." Record it and play the recording for the class.

❑ **Chapter 18**

Discussion: How does Tom prove to Aunt Polly that he loves her? How does Tom treat Becky? How does Becky get revenge?

Activities: Imagine you are Tom or Becky. Write a letter to Dear Abby for advice about your relationship. Exchange letters. Respond. Exchange back.

❑ **Chapter 19**

Discussion: What has Aunt Polly learned? How is her faith in Tom restored?

Activities: Write a letter of apology from Tom to his aunt.

❑ **Chapter 20**

Discussion: Why is Tom punished by the school master? Why doesn't he deserve his punishment? What reward does he get?

Activities: Research early schools. How were they different from today's schools? Make a list of the rules in early schools. Print them out on a computer and display them in your class.

❑ **Chapter 21**

Discussion: Why do the children want revenge on the school master? How did they get their revenge?

Activities: Construct an old fashioned schoolhouse out of popsicle sticks. Make children and the teacher out of art clay that represent the children and teacher in Tom's schoolhouse.

Tom Sawyer Chapter Activities *(cont.)*

❏ **Chapter 22**

Discussion: What organization does Tom join? What truth does Tom discover? Why is Tom unhappy with summer plans?

Activities: Make up rules for a secret organization. Draw up floor plans (either by hand or on the computer) for a secret meeting place.

❏ **Chapter 23**

Discussion: What major events happen during the trial? What decision does Tom make?

Activities: Participate in writing a trial. Participate in a trial simulation.

❏ **Chapter 24**

Discussion: How does the town react? What is Tom's fear?

Activities: Create a plan for a computer game in which Tom is trying to escape from Injun Joe. Write an article for the town newspaper concerning the events of the trial.

❏ **Chapter 25**

Discussion: Where is room number two? Why is that room important?

Activities: Draw a secret treasure map.

❏ **Chapter 26**

Discussion: What do the boys find inside room two? What do they decide to do?

Activities: Write an essay describing a hunt for buried treasure. Your teacher will hide an object somewhere in the room. Then he or she will divide you in groups and give you a list of clues. Find the objects.

❏ **Chapter 27**

Discussion: Why is Tom excited? Where do Tom and Becky go after lunch? Why do they meet and what does he want to do?

Activities: Search for pictures of caves and caverns and display in the classroom. Read about caves and caverns.

❏ **Chapter 28 to Conclusion**

Discussion: What happens to Huck? What happens to Tom and Becky?

Activities: Describe a time you were lost. Draw a picture of Tom and Becky's cave and show them a way out.

Wanted

Samuel Langhorne Clemens alias Mark Twain

Age: 163 years old as of 1998 (born in 1835)

Place of Birth: Hannibal, Missouri

Brief Description: blue eyes, white hair, white mustache, white suit

Occupations: journeyman printer, riverboat pilot, prospector, newspaper reporter, author

Wanted for: humorous writings

Famous Works:

"The Celebrated Jumping Frog of Calveras County" (1865)

Innocents Abroad (1869)

Roughing It (1872)

The Gilded Age (1873)

The Adventures of Tom Sawyer (1876)

A Tramp Abroad (1880)

The Stolen White Elephant (1882)

A Connecticut Yankee at King Arthur's Court (1889)

Tom Sawyer Abroad (1894)

Tom Sawyer, Detective (1896)

Eve's Diary (1906)

Life on the Mississippi (1883)

The Adventures of Huckleberry Finn (1885)

Make Your Own Wanted Poster

1. Decide how you want to look.

2. Select materials from the costume box or from old clothes at home.

3. Get your picture taken by yourself or in a group. (You may want to be part of a gang.)

4. Fill out the information on a sheet of paper.

5. Copy the information on posterboard.

6. Paste the picture on the board.

The Mighty Mississippi

Hernando De Soto was the first European explorer to see the muddy waters of the mighty Mississippi in 1541. With rivers from 31 states and Canada draining into its water, the Mississippi earned its name as the "Father of Waters," stretching 2,348 miles.

Although De Soto is usually credited with discovering the river, Sieur de La Salle, a French explorer, reached the mouth of the great river in 1682, and laid claim to much of its territory for France. During the 18th century, the French used the Mississippi for fur trade, establishing towns along its banks: Peoria (1680), Detroit (1701), New Orleans (1718), and St. Louis (1764).

In 1803 Napoleon sold the area between the Mississippi and the Rocky Mountains to President Thomas Jefferson. The Mississippi became part of America in this deal between France and America called the Louisiana Purchase. Instead of fur traders, the river was now full of flatboats, rafts, and heelboats carrying grain and lumber. Shortly thereafter, steamboats drifted up and down the river, filled with pleasure seekers and gamblers. During the mid-1800s, the river was filled with 3,000 steamboats and other vessels. Mark Twain spent some of his happiest days as a riverboat pilot on the Mississippi. Those carefree days soon disappeared with the Civil War. The very river that had helped the South develop industry became one of the key points of the Northern invasion.

Today, a series of dikes have been built on the river to help control the flooding and to aid today's industries that continue to thrive on the mighty river's banks.

Reading Check

1. Who was the first European explorer to see the Mississippi?
2. How many states have rivers that drain into the Mississippi?
3. What is the river's nickname?
4. Who was the first to reach the mouth of the river?
5. What was the Louisiana Purchase?
6. During the 1800s, how many steamboats traveled up and down the Mississippi?
7. What famous author was a riverboat pilot on the river?
8. How was the river used during the Civil War?
9. How was the river changed in modern times?
10. Look on the map on page 51 and list the states with rivers that drain into the Mississippi.

- -

Fold under before copying.

1. Hernando De Soto
2. 31
3. Father of Waters
4. La Salle
5. The United States bought a huge land area from France.
6. 3,000
7. Mark Twain
8. Key point of the Northern invasion
9. Dikes now control flooding.
10. Answers will vary.

Map of the Mississippi

The Mississippi River was an important part of Mark Twain's life and his novels. Below is a map of the Mississippi River and the states that it touches.

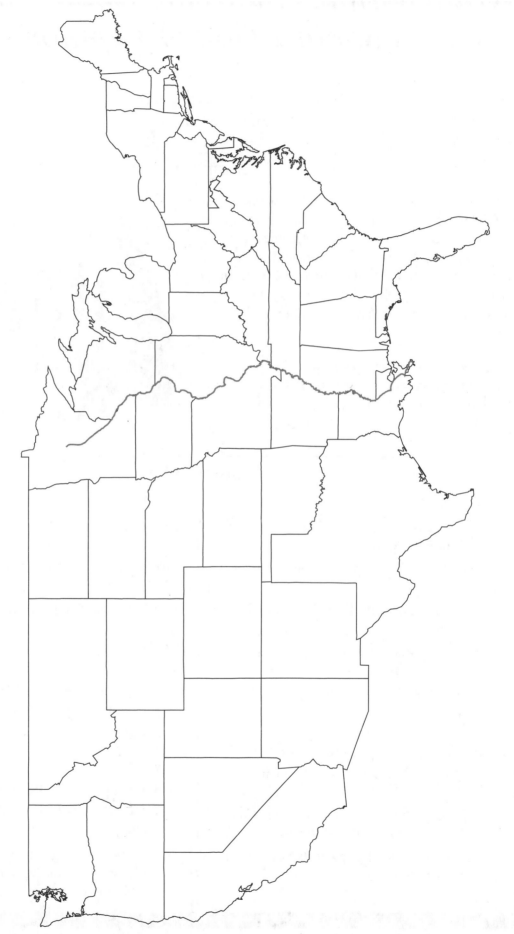

United States Supreme Court Library: Sandra Day O'Connor

by Paul J. Deegan
(Raintree Steck Vaughn, 1994)

Summary

In a court having few minorities and no women, Sandra Day O'Connor made history as the first woman ever to be appointed to the United States Supreme Court. Paul Deegan explores the life of this woman, her career, and finally her appointment to the Supreme Court. In 39 reader-friendly pages, he relates her story and the impact her appointment had on the Court and on the country.

The outline below is a suggested plan for using the various activities that are presented in this unit. You may adapt these ideas to fit your own classroom situation.

Sample Plan

Day 1

- Brainstorm functions of the U.S. Supreme Court
- Read Famous Supreme Court Justices. (pages 58–59)
- Prepare Supreme Court Bulletin Board. (pages 72–77)
- Read pages 4–10, *U.S. Supreme Court Library: Sandra Day O'Connor.*
- Begin Section Activities. (page 53)

Day 2

- Read Women in Politics. (pages 56–57)
- Discuss Contributions of Women in Politics.
- Read pages 11–21, *U.S. Supreme Court Library: Sandra Day O'Connor.*
- Participate in class project: Newsreel of the 1930s. (page 55)

Day 3

- Discuss differences in Supreme Court Procedure.
- Read pages 22–27, *U.S. Supreme Court Library: Sandra Day O'Connor.*
- Continue Section Activities. (page 53)

Day 4

- Read pages 28–31, *U.S. Supreme Court Library: Sandra Day O'Connor.*
- Continue Section Activities. (page 53)
- Complete life skills activity. (page 70)

Day 5

- Read pages 32–38, *U.S. Supreme Court Library: Sandra Day O'Connor.*
- Complete Section Activities. (page 53)
- Participate in group project: Construction of the Supreme Court Building out of newspaper and tape.

Sandra Day O'Connor Section Activities

Pages 4–10

Discussion: Where did Sandra Day O'Connor grow up? Why was attaining a good education a problem? When did she leave home? Why? What happened to her after school? Where was Sandra Day born? When? What type of life did she lead? Who was her grandfather? How did he make his money? How did the ranch get its name? Why did H.C. take his family to Los Angeles? Why didn't Harry attend Stanford? Whom did Harry marry?

Activities: Explore life on a ranch through research and/or guest speakers. View a videotape of a rodeo and write descriptive paragraphs.

Pages 11–21

Discussion: Describe Sandra's mother's education. What did she read to her daughter? Why didn't Sandra have friends her age? Why did she go to live with her grandparents? Who most influenced her life and why? When did she graduate from public high school? Describe her life at college. When she got her law degree, where did she rank in her class? Whom did she marry? Why did she have difficulty finding a job? Where did they decide to live? How many children did she have? Who became her partner? To what political party did Sandra belong? What appointment did she get in 1969? What position did she have in the Arizona legislature in 1973? Who decided to appoint Sandra Day O'Connor to the Supreme Court?

Activities: Read and/or research the lives of other women in politics. Participate in the newsreel project.

Pages 22–27

Discussion: How did conservative Republicans feel about O'Connor's appointment? What prominent Democrat praised the nomination? How did O'Connor prepare for the confirmation hearings? How did she perform during the hearings? How many committee members voted to confirm her? How many opposing votes were there in the Senate?

Activities: Make a list of all the steps Sandra Day O'Connor had to go through before she was confirmed. Look up old newspaper clippings concerning her appointment. Make a poster showing the major difference between Republicans and Democrats. Divide into groups of two. Make a tape recording of the confirmation hearings. Have one person be the interviewer and have the other be O'Connor.

Pages 28–31

Discussion: When did Sandra Day O'Connor become the first female on the Supreme Court? Describe the ceremonies. Whose chair is the ceremonial chair? Where does the newest justice sit?

Activities: Have students imagine they are being sworn in as a chief justice. Have them write about the ceremony. From the description in the book, illustrate the ceremony. Discuss what an oath means and when it might be used.

Pages 32–38

Discussion: Discuss Sandra Day O'Connor's decisions in several cases. What decision did her husband have to make? What does he do now? What misfortunes did O'Connor have to deal with in 1989? What event helped to put her life back on track?

Activities: Have the students make a time line of Sandra Day O'Connor's life. On butcher paper, illustrate contributions women have made to society. Display the paper in the hall.

Introduce Sandra Day O'Connor

Politicians are often too busy to write their own speeches. Imagine you are a speech writer for Sandra Day O'Connor. Look up information about her life in Paul J. Deegan's book, *United States Supreme Court Library: Sandra Day O'Connor*. Using those facts, write a speech introducing her to your class. While you are writing, think about the students in her audience. Try to make the speech interesting to them and still use all the important information. After you finish, your teacher may ask you to share your speech with the rest of the class.

Important Facts to Include

- Full Name:
- Born:
- Location:
- Parents:
- How did she spend her childhood?
- Who were important people in her childhood? Why?
- Schools Attended:
- Types of Jobs:
- Date she was appointed to the Supreme Court:
- Why was she appointed?
- Who appointed her?

After you finish writing your speech, you may want to use some type of visual aid to make the speech more interesting. Here are some suggestions.

- Map of El Paso
- Map of Arizona
- Drawing of Sandra Day O'Connor
- Drawing of the Supreme Court of the United States
- Drawing of Ronald Reagan
- Pictures of ranches in Texas
- Cowboy or cowgirl gear
- Drawings of schools she attended
- Pictures of her family

Tips on Making a Speech

- Establish eye contact with the audience.
- Be familiar with your speech.
- Keep your feet on the floor.
- Keep gum out of your mouth.
- Use natural gestures.
- Speak clearly.
- Practice your speech in front of a mirror or watch yourself on video tape.

Newsreel of the 1930s

Sandra Day O'Connor was born in 1930. That was an important time in the history of the United States. It was the time of the Great Depression. The Great Depression began when the stock market crashed in 1929. People panicked and began drawing all their money out of the banks. Many banks ran out of money and closed their doors.

Creating a 1930s Newsreel

Before television, news was reported on newsreels in motion pictures. These were black-and-white films shown at the local theater, concerning the events of the week. Learn about the 1930s and then create a class newsreel to share with other members of your school. (A video camera will do a good job.)

❑ Begin by watching a film about life in the 1930s.

　　Suggestions: (See bibliography, page 79.)
　　It's a Wonderful Life
　　The Grapes of Wrath

❑ Interview grandparents or other people in the community who were alive in the 1930s.

❑ Make reports on famous writers of the 1930s.

　　(W.H. Auden, Noel Coward, T.S. Eliot, William Faulkner, Robert Frost, D.H. Lawrence, Sinclair Lewis, Katherine Anne Porter)

❑ Dress like famous people of that era.

　　(Charlie Chaplin, Marlene Dietrich, Greta Garbo, Alfred Hitchcock, Wallace Berry, Howard Hughes, John Wayne, Albert Einstein, Sigmund Freud, Albert Schweitzer)

❑ Listen to popular songs of the time.

　　("Georgia on My Mind," "I Got Rhythm," "Three Little Words," "Time on My Hands," "Walkin' My Baby Back Home," "Body and Soul")

❑ Look at old newspaper articles and read about important events of the time.

　　(Photo flashbulb invented; Pittsburgh wins Rose Bowl; Philadelphia wins World Series; Gallant Fox wins Preakness, Belmont Stakes, and Kentucky Derby; Charles Evans Hughes is appointed Chief Justice of the Supreme Court; Congress forms the Veteran's Administration)

❑ When the research is complete, create a newsreel telling about events and people of the 1930s.

❑ Donate the reel to history classes in the school or to the school library.

Women in Politics

Today, women often take their rights for granted. Women have not always been treated equally, however. At one time, women were not allowed to wear pants, to vote, or to work. Following are some women who became important political figures. They fought for many of the freedoms that women enjoy today.

Amelia Bloomer (1818–1894)

Amelia Bloomer got involved in women's rights at the request of her husband. Born in Homer, New York, in 1818, Amelia Bloomer became involved in women's rights after her husband encouraged her to write. She published a magazine on women's rights called *Lily*.

Although she made a contribution with her writing, she is best known for her clothing. Instead of the long dresses and uncomfortable clothes of the day, Amelia suggested that women wear short skirts and trousers gathered at the ankles—bloomers.

Susan Brounell Anthony (1820–1906)

Susan B. Anthony was born in Adams, Massachusetts, to Quaker parents. She did something women of that time would never think of doing: she voted in 1872. Since it was illegal for women to vote, she was arrested and fined $100—which she never paid. In 1892 she became the President of the American Women's Suffrage Association. Fourteen years after her death, women were given the right to vote.

Harriet Elizabeth Beecher Stowe (1811–1896)

When Abraham Lincoln met Harriet Beecher Stowe, he said "So you're the little woman who wrote the book that made this great war." Even though Harriet Beecher Stowe was not really responsible for the Civil War, she did stir up antislavery sentiment with her book *Uncle Tom's Cabin*. She was born in Litchfield, Connecticut, and was never exposed to slavery until she moved to Cincinnati, Ohio, where her father was president of Lane Theological Seminary. Slavery was common across the Ohio River in Kentucky. After she married, she moved to Maine where she began writing her novel, *Uncle Tom's Cabin*, in between caring for the needs of her six children. The novel first appeared in the abolitionist journal *National Era*. Later it was published in book form, selling 300,000 copies in the first year. Ten years later, the book had been translated into 20 languages and performed as a play on stages across the United States and in Europe. Other works by Mrs. Stowe include *Dred: A Tale of the Great Dismal Swamp* (1856), *The Minister's Wooing* (1859), and *Oldtown Folks* (1869).

Jane Addams (1860–1935)

At the age of 27, Jane Addams toured Europe and discovered the idea of British settlement houses. These houses were places where the poor could leave their children for education and care. Ms. Addams took this idea back to America, establishing Hull House in Chicago in 1889. This house became a model for other houses. Soon there were hundreds of these houses established in the slums of America's cities. After the success of Hull House, Jane Addams became an advocate for the foreign-born poor. She also became active in the women's rights movement and influential in international peace efforts, serving as chairman of the Women's Peace Party and president of the Women's International League for Peace and Freedom. In 1931 she was named co-recipient of the Nobel Peace Prize. Along with her other activities, she also wrote two books: *The Spirit of Youth and the City Streets* (1909) and *Twenty Years at Hull House* (1910).

Women in Politics *(cont.)*

Eleanor T. (Anna) Roosevelt (1884–1962)

Eleanor Roosevelt was one of the most dynamic first ladies in history. She was born in New York City in 1884 and educated in Europe. Eventually, she married her distant cousin who was to be the 32nd President of the United States. She had six children and still found time to travel with her wheelchair-bound husband during his presidency. She listened to the people and fought for the rights of the common man, including African Americans and women. She wrote about issues concerning the common man in her daily newspaper column, "My Day."

In 1945 after her husband died, Eleanor continued her involvement in politics by becoming a representative to the United Nations. It was there that she helped create the Declaration of Human Rights. She also helped reform the Democratic Party in New York, remained active in social issues, and wrote autobiographical books. When she died in 1962, her death was mourned around the world.

Pauline Cushman (1835–1893)

An actress born in New Orleans, Pauline Cushman played the greatest role of her life as a commissioned Union spy during the Civil War. When her real identity was finally discovered in 1863, she was arrested and sentenced to hang. However, in a quick retreat, the Confederacy left her behind to be rescued by Union soldiers. After her escape from death, she toured the country in a Union uniform, describing her adventures. Finally, she went West to operate a chain of hotels, losing all of her earnings and dying as a poor scrubwoman.

Other Women in Politics

If you are interested in reading more about women in politics, here is a list of women you may want to research.

- Emma Hart Willard
- Mildred Helen McAfee
- Mary Lyon
- Anne Mae Hays
- Margaret Chase Smith
- Hillary Clinton
- Diane Feinstein
- Kaye Bailey Hutchins
- Nancy Kassebaum

- Shirley Chisholm
- Dolley Madison
- Mary Elizabeth Lease
- Sarah Moore Grimke
- Ida Minerva Tarbell
- Geraldine Ferraro
- Barbara Boxer
- Anne Richards
- Christine Todd Whitman

Famous Supreme Court Justices

Earl Warren

As Chief Justice of the Supreme Court during an exciting but controversial time in our country, Earl Warren had to make many difficult decisions between 1953 and 1969. He was born on March 19, 1891, in Los Angeles, California. He grew up in Bakersfield, however, where the images of crime made an impression on him. After attending the University of California at Berkeley and its law school, he served in the army for a very brief time. After the army, he joined the district attorney's office in Alameda County for 18 years. A survey was conducted during that time, and Warren was considered to be the best district attorney in the United States. In 1938 he ran for attorney general of California and in 1942 was elected governor. He helped to secure Dwight Eisenhower's nomination for president. In turn, President Eisenhower nominated him Chief Justice of the Supreme Court. His philosophy was a common sense approach. He believed in fairness and the protection of individual rights in deciding cases.

Oliver Wendell Holmes

Nominated by President Theodore Roosevelt on August 11, 1902, Oliver Wendell Holmes served on the Supreme Court for 30 years. During that time, he wrote 873 opinions, more than any other justice. He believed that judges needed to be impartial and that the courts were an experiment in "peaceful evolution" (instead of fighting, parties were to settle disagreements with a fair trial).

Holmes was born in Boston, Massachusetts, March 8, 1841. His father was a physician and lecturer. He enjoyed talking and writing light verse. Holmes' mother was born Amelia Lee Jackson. She was the daughter of a lawyer and judge. Marrying late, she devoted her life to her husband and three children. Oliver was her favorite. His family sent him to private schools and eventually to Harvard. Growing up, he was greatly influenced by great minds such as John Ruskin, Ralph Waldo Emerson, and Thomas Carlyle.

In July 1861, Holmes enlisted in the federal army. He was wounded three times and was ill much of the time. When he was offered a post as aide to General Horatio Wright, he hesitated taking it. But during the winter, he had few responsibilities and spent his time writing about his ideas on war.

Finally, he decided to leave the army. Returning to Boston, he attended Harvard Law School and was admitted to the bar in 1867. Shortly thereafter, he decided to give up his practice and write articles and reviews for James Kent's *Commentaries on American Law* and the *American Law Review*.

In 1872 he married Fanny Dixwell and joined a Boston law firm. She became very ill with rheumatic fever, and for awhile he devoted himself to her care and to his law career. Eventually, he began writing again. By his fortieth birthday, he had published one of his most important works—*The Common Law*, a book of essays about common law. After the publication of *The Common Law*, Holmes taught at Harvard Law School for a semester before he was appointed to the Supreme Court. He served on the Supreme Court until an illness in the summer of 1931, which resulted in his resignation. He died of pneumonia three years later on March 6, 1935.

Famous Supreme Court Justices (cont.)

Thurgood Marshall

Working as a slave, Thurgood Marshall's great grandfather probably never imagined his great grandson would be the first African American to serve on the United States Supreme Court. Thurgood Marshall was born in Baltimore, Maryland, on July 2, 1908. His father was a dining car waiter, and his mother was a school teacher. In 1930 he earned his degree from Lincoln University. He became interested in civil rights at Howell, where he graduated first in his class in 1933.

After his graduation, he became actively involved in civil rights issues, serving as a lawyer for the National Association for the Advancement of Colored People (NAACP) and director of the NAACP Legal Defense and Educational Fund. John F. Kennedy nominated Marshall to be circuit judge on the U.S. Court of Appeals for the Second Circuit in 1961. He spent four years on the circuit. Then, in 1965 President Lyndon Johnson named Marshall to be the first African American solicitor general of the United States. Two years later, Johnson appointed him to the Supreme Court. During his time on the court, Marshall continued to be concerned with civil rights, and he also became actively opposed to the death penalty.

John Marshall

John Marshall is known as "the great Chief Justice." He was appointed to the Supreme Court by President John Adams on January 20, 1801. The oldest of 15 children, Marshall grew up on the northwestern frontier of Virginia. It was there he acquired many of his conservative values which he brought to the Supreme Court.

In 1783 he married Betsy Ambler. They had 10 children, four of whom died before adulthood. He had only two years of formal education. His father taught him math and English and introduced him to politics through Blackstone's *Commentaries on the Laws of England* (1765). When the Revolutionary War began, he and his father were among the first to enlist. During this time, he developed fierce patriotism and an admiration for George Washington. By 1780 he began his study of law by attending a law lecture at William and Mary. After a brief time, he began his practice of the law. With little formal training, but with a sharp mind, he easily rose to the top of the Richmond bar.

He served on Virginia's Council of State (1782–1784) and in the House of Delegates (1782, 1784–1785, 1787–1788, and 1795). He was offered the offices of the U.S. Attorney General, Minister to France, and Associate Justice of the Supreme Court. He turned all of these opportunities down for financial reasons. After returning from a diplomatic mission to France, he was asked to serve in Congress (1799–1800). He also served as Secretary of State before becoming Chief Justice on March 5, 1801. One of his first tasks was to strengthen the Court by getting permission for the Court to speak in one voice. By the end of his term, he had become the role model for Chief Justice of the Supreme Court.

Chart of Supreme Court Justices

Since 1789, Presidents have been appointing Supreme Court Justices. This chart includes a list of all the justices, the years they were appointed, and the Presidents who appointed them.

President	Year	Chief Justices	Associate Justices
George Washington	1789	John Jay	John Rutledge
			William Cushing
			James Wilson
			John Blair
	1790		James Iredell
	1791		Thomas Johnson
	1793		William Paterson
	1795	John Rutledge	
	1796	Oliver Ellsworth	Samuel Chase
John Adams	1798		Bushrod Washington
	1799		Alfred Moore
Thomas Jefferson	1801	John Marshall	
	1804		William Johnson
	1806		Brockholst Livingston
	1807		Thomas Todd
James Madison	1811		Gabriel Duvall
			Joseph Story
James Monroe	1823		Smith Thompson
John Quincy Adams	1826		Robert Trimble
Andrew Jackson	1829		John Mclean
	1830		Henry Baldwin
	1835		James M. Wayne
	1836	Roger B. Taney	Philip P. Barbour
Martin Van Buren	1837		John Catron
	1841		Peter V. Daniel
John Tyler	1845		Samuel Nelson
James K. Polk	1845		Levi Woodbury
	1846		Robert C. Grier
Millard Fillmore	1851		Benjamin R. Curtis
Franklin Pierce	1853		John A. Campbell
James Buchanan	1858		Nathan Clifford
Abraham Lincoln	1862		Noah H. Swayne
			Samuel F. Miller
			David Davis
	1863		Stephen J. Field
	1864	Salmon P. Chase	
Ulysses S. Grant	1870		William Strong
			Joseph P. Bradley
	1872		Ward Hunt
	1874	Morrison R. Waite	
Rutherford Hayes	1877		John Marshall Harlan
	1880		William B. Woods
James A. Garfield	1881		Stanley Matthews
Chester A. Arthur	1881		Horace Gray
	1882		Samuel Blatchford
Grover Cleveland	1888	Melville W. Fuller	Lucius Q.C. Lamer
Benjamin Harrison	1889		David J. Brewer
	1890		Henry B. Brown

Chart of Supreme Court Justices *(cont.)*

President	Date	Chief Justices	Associate Justices
	1892		George Shiras, Jr.
	1893		Howell Jackson
Grover Cleveland	1894		Edward Douglass White
	1895		Rufus W. Peckham
William McKinley	1898		Joseph McKenna
Theodore Roosevelt	1902		Oliver Wendell Holmes
			William R. Day
	1906		William H. Moody
William H. Taft	1909		Horace H. Lurton
	1910	Edward D. White	Charles Evans Hughes
			Willis Van Devanter
			Joseph R. Lamar
	1912		Mahlon Pitney
Woodrow Wilson	1914		James C. McReynolds
	1916		Louis D. Brandeis
			John H. Clarke
Warren G. Harding	1921	William H. Taft	
	1922		George Sutherland
	1922		Pierce Butler
	1923		Edward T. Sanford
Calvin Coolidge	1925		Harlan Fiske Stone
Herbert Hoover	1930	Charles E. Hughes	Owen J. Roberts
	1932		Benjamin N. Cardozo
Franklin Roosevelt	1937		Hugo L. Black
	1938		Stanley Forman Reed
	1939		Felix Frankfurter
			William O. Douglas
	1940		Frank Murphy
	1941	Harlan Fiske Stone	James F. Byrnes
			Robert H. Jackson
	1943		Wiley B. Rutledge
	1945		Harold H. Burton
Harry S. Truman	1946	Fred M. Vinson	
	1949		Thomas C. Clark
			Sherman Minton
Dwight D. Eisenhower	1953	Earl Warren	
	1955		John Marshall Harlan
	1956		William J. Brennan, Jr
	1957		Charles E. Whittaker
	1958		Potter Stewart
John F. Kennedy	1962		Byron R. White
			Arthur J. Goldberg
Lyndon B. Johnson	1965		Abe Fortas
	1967		Thurgood Marshall
Richard M. Nixon	1969	Warren E. Burger	
	1970		Harry A. Blackmun
	1971		Lewis F. Powell, Jr.
			William H. Rehnquist
Gerald Ford	1975		John P. Stevens
Ronald Reagan	1981		Sandra Day O'Connor
	1986	William Rehnquist	Antonin Scalia
	1988		Anthony M. Kennedy
George Bush	1990		David H. Souter
	1991		Clarence Thomas

Supreme Court Procedures

The Supreme Court is run differently than other federal courts. The justices begin their work year on the first Monday in October. They continue working until the last decision of the term is made. Over 4,000 requests for appeals are made to the Supreme Court each year, but only around 150 cases are actually heard. If the case is not heard, the decision of the lower court stands. Four of the nine justices must vote to hear a case before it is put on the docket. Once the decision for review is made, the counsels from both sides are notified. At that point, the lawyers for both sides file briefs that the justices study.

A day in the Supreme Court is much different from a day in a lower federal court. Nine justices file into the courtroom, instead of one. The Chief Justice sits to the far left. The other justices sit in order of appointment from left to right. Each side is allotted 30 minutes to defend the case. The justices often stop the attorneys to ask them questions. Then, each justice writes his or her opinion. Finally, the justices have a confidential meeting on Friday to discuss their opinions. One person on the side with the most votes writes an opinion. Sometimes, justices on the side with the least votes also write an opinion. After reading the majority opinion, justices will sometimes write concurring opinions, opinions that agree with the majority opinion and sometimes make suggestions for information they would like included. Nothing is revealed to the public until the final decisions are announced.

Once a decision is made, it can be overturned by Congress through establishment of new laws. It also may be overturned by an amendment to the Constitution, and finally the Court, itself, sometimes reverses a decision.

Comprehension Check

Answer "T" for true and "F" for false.

_____ 1. The Supreme Court is run the same as other courts.

_____ 2. The justices begin work on the first Monday in October.

_____ 3. Four thousand cases are heard per year.

_____ 4. Each lawyer has 30 minutes to present his or her case.

_____ 5. No witnesses are called during the trials.

_____ 6. The justices sit in the order of seniority.

_____ 7. All nine justices have to vote to hear a case for that case to be heard.

_____ 8. Majority opinions are written by at least one justice.

_____ 9. Laws made by the Supreme Court may never be overturned.

_____10. Friday discussions among the justices are videotaped to serve as permanent records of the meetings.

Supreme Court Meeting Places

These are pictures of the meeting places of the Supreme Court. The most recent is the Supreme Court Building.

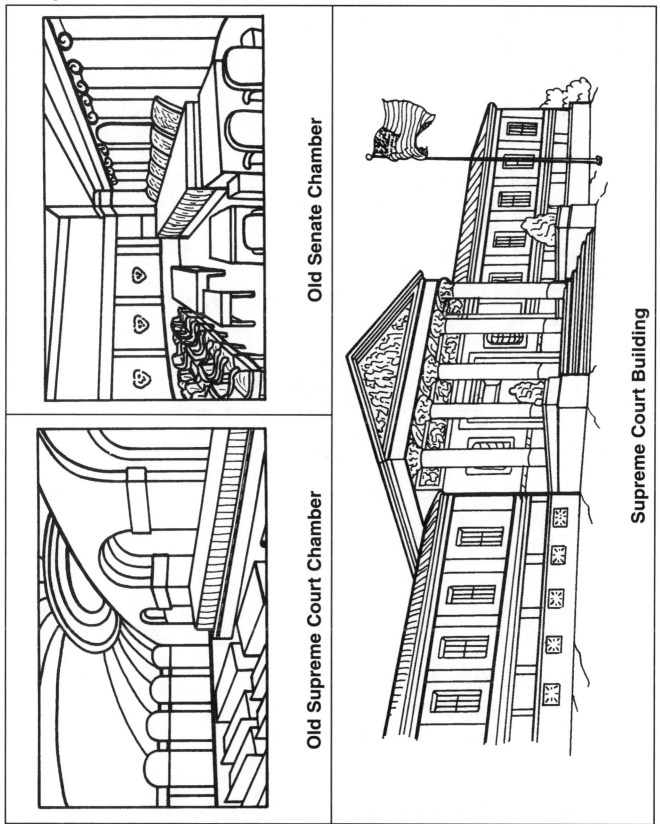

Old Senate Chamber

Old Supreme Court Chamber

Supreme Court Building

Supreme Court Trivia

Research these questions about the Supreme Court. Check your answers by looking on the bottom of the page.

1. Where was the first session of the Supreme Court held?
2. Who was the youngest appointed justice?
3. Who swore in the most presidents?
4. Who was the longest-living justice?
5. Who was the only justice to serve on the Supreme Court and as President of the United States?
6. Name five associate justices who became Chief Justices.
7. Who was the first African American justice?
8. Who appointed the first woman justice?
9. Who sits farthest away from the Chief Justice? Why?
10. What color robes do the justices wear?
11. Who is the only justice to have his face on American currency?
12. What bill is it?
13. What type of promise do the justices make during their formal ceremony?
14. What type of pens do the justices use?
15. What justice served the longest term?

Trivia Answers

1. Royal Exchange building
2. Joseph Story (appointed in 1812 at the age of 33)
3. Roger B. Taney
4. Stanley F. Reed
5. William H. Taft
6. John Rutledge, Edward D. White, Charles E. Hughes, Harlan F. Stone, and William H. Rehnquist
7. Thurgood Marshall
8. Ronald Reagan
9. The junior justice, seniority seating
10. Black
11. Salmon Chase
12. $10,000
13. Oath
14. Quill
15. William O. Douglas (served from 1939 until 1975—36 years)

Using Drama in the Classroom

One of the most exciting and interesting ways of learning is through the use of drama in the classroom. It is not only fun for the students but also fun for the teacher. The following suggestions may be changed or modified to fit your classroom.

1. **Collect all the materials you need ahead of time.**

   Tell the students that at the end of the unit, they will have their day in court. Brainstorm a list of materials they think they will need. You may want to add to or delete from the list later. After you edit the list, place a copy on the bulletin board and ask students to sign up to bring in different items. For example, if you need a gavel, a wooden meat tenderizer is a good substitute. If you need a robe for the judge, a choir robe may do.

2. **Create a prop box.**

   Clean out a closet or visit the local thrift store. Fill the box with shoes, wigs, hats, suits, dresses, old costume jewelry. Your students will probably have some of these at home, too.

3. **Send a letter to parents.**

   Parents often get as excited as the students if you let them know a schedule of the exciting activities in this unit. You may get some volunteers or some donations.

4. **Give the students an interest survey.**

   Divide the students into groups according to their answers instead of letting them select groups.

5. **Hand each group a task list.**

   Tell them that they will be graded on the completion of the task according to the criteria on the grade sheet.

6. **Set a realistic time.**

   You may even let students help set the time. They may be more willing to follow the schedule if they help set it.

7. **Give the class clear directions the day before.**

   Tell them where their group will be, where the directions will be, and what will be expected of them.

8. **Move from group to group to monitor noise and progress.**

   You may want to set up a reward system so that the groups who have the least noise or mess win a prize or get a bonus on the project.

Southern Dialect

Although English is our common language, different areas of the United States have different dialects. Dialects are variations in our language that reflect the culture and heritage of an area. The characters in Mark Twain's *Tom Sawyer* speak with a Southern dialect. Try to match words commonly found in a Southern dialect with their correct meaning.

_____	1. cooter	a. about to do something
_____	2. wiggler	b. peanut
_____	3. gwine	c. dragonfly
_____	4. heern tell	d. messy
_____	5. on account of	e. a large amount
_____	6. mosquito hawk	f. going
_____	7. goober	g. all of you
_____	8. gaumy	h. throat
_____	9. hidy	i. throw
_____	10. y'all	j. turtle
_____	11. goozle	k. bait worm
_____	12. passle	l. to hear about
_____	13. chuck	m. grandfather
_____	14. big daddy	n. because
_____	15. fixing to	o. hello

Examine your own dialect. Make a list of words or expressions you hear that may be unusual to your area.

1. _____   6. _____

2. _____   7. _____

3. _____   8. _____

4. _____   9. _____

5. _____   10. _____

Mississippi Math

Tom has grown up on the Mississippi watching steamboats roll up and down the river. Read and solve the following problems about steamboats. Work the problems in order since they are connected.

1. Tom enjoys watching the steamboats speed down the river. He knows that each one carries 500 bales of cotton. On Monday, he counts 23 boats. On Tuesday, he counts 14 boats. On Wednesday, Thursday, and Friday, he counts 11 boats per day. How many bales of cotton were shipped to market on how many boats?

2. Tom knows that a steamboat engine is fueled by wood. He also knows that one cord of wood provides enough fuel to travel 2 ½ miles going down the river. How many cords of wood are needed to travel 1,000 miles?

3. When a steamboat travels up river, it needs 2 ½ times as many cords of wood as are needed to travel down the river. How many cords of wood are required to fuel the boat the same distance (1,000 miles) up river?

4. How many cords of wood are needed to reach the first refueling stop 100 miles up river?

5. How many cords of wood are needed to make the round trip of 2,000 miles?

6. Tom also enjoys watching the steamboats race down the river. The fastest time recorded for the 1,000 mile trip down the river is 120 hours. How many days equal 120 hours?

7. The trip up the river takes 2 ½ times as long. How many hours does the trip up the river take?

8. How many days does the trip up the river require?

9. Racing requires more fuel than a normal trip. If the race down the river requires 2 ¼ as much fuel, how many cords of wood are needed to race 1,000 miles down the river?

10. A 1,000 mile race up the river requires 3 ¾ times as much fuel as the race down the river. How many cords of wood are needed to race 1,000 miles up the river?

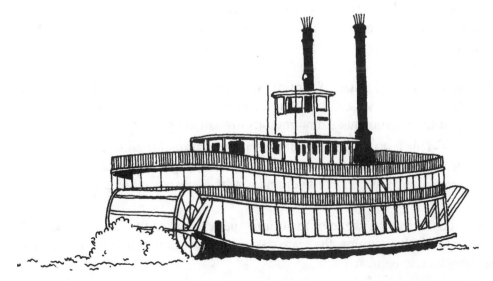

Bloodstains

Bloodstains are an important part of a criminal investigation. Experts match criminal to crime through DNA testing. Blood spatters tell an expert how the victim moved, if the assailant was injured, and how the assailant moved.

What makes blood different? Red blood cells differ under microscopic examination.

- Mammals' red blood cells are circular and have no nucleus. Camels and llamas are the only mammals that are different.

- Non-mammals have oval red blood cells with a visible nucleus.

Experiment

If your school has access to microscopes and laboratory-approved slides of different types of blood cells, you might examine some and then draw what you see. Check your drawings to see if they show the characteristics mentioned above.

If your drawings are accurate, make transparencies to show to the class on an overhead projector.

Using Blood Samples as Evidence

When a forensic team investigates a murder, they determine if any blood is present at the scene of the crime. They not only look at the clues the victim's blood gives them, but they also look for traces of the murderer's blood. If the guilty party is scratched or cut, traces of that person's blood might help determine the murderer.

A forensic team has a variety of methods of testing blood at the scene of a crime. The following are some of the most commonly used tests:

1. **Benzidine Test**—This is a chemical test which reacts to traces of blood. The problem with this test is that the chemical also gives the same reaction when testing fresh fruit or milk.

2. **Reduced Phenolphthalein Test**—When this chemical reacts with blood, it turns rose colored. Unfortunately, it will turn rose colored with a variety of other substances, too. However, its usefulness is that if there is not a rose-colored reaction with a substance, the substance is definitely not blood.

3. **Leuco-Malachite Test**—Instead of turning rose, this substance turns green if it is blood. This test is reliable. However, it is so sensitive that the investigator has to make sure that no trace of blood is left on any of the instruments from previous investigations.

4. **Luminol Test**—This test is especially helpful if the criminal tried to clean up the area after the crime. The team turns out the lights after mixing the sample with a mixture of sodium carbonate, sodium perborate, and 3-aminophtalhydrazide. If the substance being tested is blood, it will glow in the dark!

If the sample tests positive at the scene of the crime, the team takes the sample back to the lab for further tests. Sometimes that requires the team to cut out a portion of a wall or a section of carpet containing the substance to be tested.

DNA Testing

You are unique. No one is exactly like you. What makes you different from anyone else? Your environment has a lot to do with who you are. Where you live, what you experience, and what you are taught help determine who you are. In addition to environment, heredity helps determine who you are. Inside the cells in your body is a genetic code which helps determine whether your hair is black or brown, your eyes are blue or green, or you are short or tall. Your genetic code is different from anyone else's code.

It is this code that investigators are now beginning to use as evidence in criminal cases. This type of testing, called DNA fingerprinting, has been used only since 1988. Since that time, it has helped clear over 2,000 suspects of crimes they never committed.

Every person has DNA (Deoxyribonucleic Acid). It is found in your chromosomes. Most people have 46 chromosomes. You inherited 23 from each one of your parents. Each DNA molecule is made up of four bases of nucleotides: Adenine (A), Cytosine (C), Guanine (G), and Thymine (T). These bases join together in strands and wrap around each other in a structure called a double helix. When these four bases line up in this structure, they may be in any order. The second strand is determined by the order of the first strand. Adenine only lines up in front of Thymine, and Cytosine lines up in front of Guanine. It is this order that determines your genetic coding and makes you different from everyone else. A complete copy of this code is found in every one of your cells. Consequently, if a criminal leaves evidence behind, such as a strand of hair or a drop of blood, investigators can examine that evidence for DNA.

Supreme Court Decision

Is it legal to take a blood sample from a suspect, or does it violate the Fifth Amendment against self-incrimination? In the case of *Schmerber v. State of California*, the Supreme Court ruled that it did not violate the Fifth Amendment. The judges stated that self-incrimination involves oral testimony and that taking blood or hair samples did not fall under that category. What do you think?

Ethics . . . in and out of Court

Ethics are moral principals. They make up your beliefs of right and wrong. To ensure that lawyers practiced ethics, the American Bar Association was formed in 1878. They were 75 practicing lawyers who volunteered their time. They established a code of professional ethics in 1908. They also established some criteria for becoming a lawyer, which included three years of law school and passing a state bar exam.

Why do you think the American Bar Association might be an important organization? Do you believe ethics are an important part of the school environment? Following are some situations involving ethical choices. Your teacher may put you in groups or may ask you to complete the assignment independently. Read the situations and write your reactions to each one.

Situation #1

Your best friend steals money from another student. You see him or her. What do you believe you should do? Would you risk losing your friendship by turning your friend in?

Would you talk to your friend and try to get him or her to return the money? How would you handle the situation? What do you believe is the right thing to do? Would you do what you believed was right?

Situation #2

Some students are spreading rumors that there is going to be a fight after school. You know the students who are going to fight. You know one has threatened to kill the other one.

You really believe the situation could be dangerous. What are you going to do? Why do you believe you would react in that way?

Situation #3

You know that another student is having a lot of problems. That student seems to be unhappy all the time. You don't really like the person, but you are worried, nevertheless. What will you do? What do you believe is right? Will you do what you believe is right?

Situation #4

One of your friends is in the habit of making jokes that hurt others' feelings. You really don't like the jokes either. Are you going to do anything about it? Why or why not?

Situation #5

You haven't studied for a test, and you are in danger of failing the class. The smartest student in class sits right in front of you. Today, you notice you can see that person's tests answers. You don't think you will get caught by the teacher. Are you going to copy the paper? Why or why not?

Creative Writing Assignments

Tom Sawyer

1. Update the trial in *Tom Sawyer*. Write a modern day version of the trial.
2. Imagine you are a riverboat pilot. Describe an adventure.
3. Write Injun Joe's side of the story.
4. Transport Aunt Polly into the 1990s. Describe her reaction to what she sees.
5. Write a story entitled "Mystery on the Riverboat."
6. What do think Tom and Huck are like when they grow up? Describe them as adults.
7. Sid is jealous of Tom and believes Twain should write a book about him. Help Sid with his letter to Mark Twain.
8. Becky's character is never fully developed in *The Adventures of Tom Sawyer*. Imagine Becky kept a diary. What would it say? Make entries in Becky's diary.
9. Tom grew up in the 1800s in the rural South. He spent his day wandering the riverbanks and getting into mischief. Enjoy a day in Tom's environment. Write about what you did.
10. The boys witness a murder in the graveyard. Make up a mystery story that begins with a midnight trip to the graveyard.

Sandra Day O'Connor

1. You are a detective. Using DNA testing, you are able to solve a case that occurred in the 1930s. Give the history of the case and tell how you solved the crime.
2. You are a reporter in Sandra Day O'Connor's hometown. Write a newspaper article describing her appointment.
3. How do you think Sandra Day O'Connor felt on appointment day? Imagine you are she, and write what you are thinking.
4. Interview Ronald Reagan, asking him about his decision to appoint the first woman to the Supreme Court.
5. Read about a famous Supreme Court decision. Make up the dialogue you think occurred among the chief justices.

Legal System

1. You are a lawyer who finds out the person you are defending is guilty. Write your reaction. What do you decide to do and why?
2. You are part of the forensic team called to investigate a murder. Describe your job and how you help solve the crime.
3. Read about a famous trial. Discuss the evidence and whether you believe the trial was a fair one.
4. Read a Supreme Court Decision. Imagine you are one of the justices and write your opinion.
5. Read a recent newspaper article about a crime. Describe whether the defendant is guilty or innocent based on the facts as reported. Follow the case until its conclusion.
6. You are a legal secretary for a famous lawyer. Your boss has asked you to meet him at 304 Apple Lane at 8:00 P.M. When you arrive, you witness a crime in progress. Tell your story.
7. At a school basketball game, one of the students disappears. You collect the clues and find the student. Explain what happened.
8. You are a member of a jury that can't agree on a verdict. You have been locked in a room for days. Describe the other jurors and what finally happens.

Bulletin Board Ideas

One of the most often overlooked educational tools in the classroom is the bulletin board. When students are allowed to participate in creating the bulletin board, it becomes a display case for their work and their creativity. Instead of spending hours alone cutting out pictures and letters, try this idea with your students.

❏ **Divide the class into groups of two or three.**

❏ **Give each group a copy of the Chart of Supreme Court Justices. (page 60 and 61)**

❏ **Ask them to select a chief justice.**

❏ **After selecting their justice, the group needs to research the person and fill out the "I believe . . ." card with a statement from his or her background, reflecting important ideas held or promoted by this justice. On the back of the card, add important biographical data, including education and experience.**

❏ **The group should then look at the sketch of the justice they selected.**

❏ **They should decide on one member of the group who will play the part of the chief justice.**

❏ **Using materials from the costume box and light theatrical makeup, the students should recreate the justice.**

❏ **Using an instant camera, take a picture of the student.**

   Hint: **If two students in the group want to be made up, let one of them be the president who appoints the chief justice.**

❏ **The students should mount the picture in the frame and put it with others on the bulletin board in chronological or alphabetical order. The "I believe . . ." card and name of the chief justice should go under the picture.**

Bulletin Board Ideas (cont.)

Cut out the names of the following justices and place them under the correct pictures on the bulletin board. All but two of these are chief justices.

John Jay
John Rutledge
Oliver Ellsworth
John Marshall
Roger Brooke Taney
Salmon P. Chase
Morrison R. Waite
Melville W. Fuller
Edward Douglass White
William Howard Taft
Charles Evans Hughes
Harlan Fiske Stone
Fred M. Vinson
Earl Warren
Warren E. Burger
William H. Rehnquist
Charles Evans Whitaker
Wiley Blount Rutledge, Jr.

Bulletin Board Ideas *(cont.)*

Select your justice from this group of sketches.

John Jay

John Rutledge

Oliver Ellsworth

John Marshall

Roger Brooke Taney

Salmon P. Chase

74

Bulletin Board Ideas *(cont.)*

Morrison R. Waite

Melville W. Fuller

Edward Douglass White

William Howard Taft

Charles Evans Hughes

Harlan Fiske Stone

Bulletin Board Ideas *(cont.)*

Frederick M. Vinson

Earl Warren

Warren E. Burger

Willam H. Rehnquist

Charles Evans Whitaker

Wiley Blount Rutledge, Jr.

Bulletin Board Ideas *(cont.)*

United States of America
Supreme Court

Chief Justice

Born:_____ Died:_____

I believe . . .

More Bulletin Board Ideas

❏ Draw a picture of the crime scene before the simulation. Make a bulletin board out of it. Offer a prize for the person who discovers the murderer based on the clues.

❏ During the simulation, have a student be the photographer. Put the pictures of the simulation on the bulletin board.

❏ Post a series of mystery pictures on the bulletin board. Change them at the end of each day, leaving the ones that went unsolved on the bulletin board for the next day.

❏ Have the students write mystery stories. Use half the bulletin board to display writings. Use the other half to display illustrations of their stories.

❏ Use newspaper stories as the background of your bulletin board. Have the students' opinions about those stories mounted on black construction paper and placed on top of the newspaper. Have a contest on the computer concerning the 3-D office design on computer. Display these designs on the bulletin board.

❏ After the students complete their activity on planet Zota, let them draw what their world will look like. Ask them to print out the laws they selected on the computer. Mount these projects.

❏ Research the South and do a bulletin board based on that theme. It could even include recipes, words from spirituals, poems, etc. Divide the students into groups and let them research one aspect of the South. Based on that research, make a contribution to the bulletin board.

❏ Use your bulletin board as an opinion center. Put a topic across the top of the board every day. Divide the board in two: Response and Counter Response. Allow students to post opinions about the topic on the bulletin board. After reading the opinions, other students may respond and post their opinions.

❏ Make a large class chart of the Tom Sawyer Chapter Activities. Give each group a section or chapter to illustrate and display on the board.

❏ Share the research on women in politics. Vote on the women who made the biggest contributions. Make a bulletin board honoring these women.

❏ Divide the chapters among the groups. Have them do a comic book summary of a chapter. Place all the chapters together and display them on the bulletin board.

Bibliography

Fiction

Twain, Mark. *The Adventures of Tom Sawyer*. HarperCollins, 1997.

Nonfiction

Bailey, F. Lee. *To Be a Trial Lawyer*. John Wiley & Son, Inc., 1985.

Beaudry, Jo and Lynne Ketchum. *Carla Goes to Court*. Human Sciences Press, Inc., 1987.

Berry, Joy. *Laws That Relate to Kids in the Community*. Children's Press, 1987.

Calvi, James V. and Susan Coleman. *American Law & Legal Systems*. Prentice Hall, 1992.

Deegan, Paul J. *United States Supreme Court Library: Sandra Day O'Connor*. Raintree Steck Vaughn, 1994.

Family Encyclopedia of American History. Reader's Digest, Inc., 1975.

Gifis, Steven H. *Law Dictionary*. Barron's, 1991.

Grun, Bernard. *The Timetables of History*. Simon & Schuster, 1991.

Hall, Kermit L. *The Oxford Companion to the Supreme Court*. Oxford Univ. Press, 1992.

Hornung, Clarence P. *The Way It Was in the South*. Smithmark, 1992.

Kurkland, Michael. *How to Solve a Murder: The Forensic Handbook*. Simon & Schuster Macmillan, 1995.

McLynn, Frank. *Famous Trials: Cases That Made History*. Reader's Digest, 1995.

Roth, Martin. *The Writer's Complete Crime Reference Book*. Writer's Digest, 1993.

Success with Words. Reader's Digest, 1983.

Wingate, Anne, Ph D. *Scene of the Crime: A Writer's Guide to Crime-Scene Investigations*. Writer's Digest Books, 1992.

Wilson, Charles Reagan & William Ferris. *Encyclopedia of Southern Culture*. University of North Carolina Press, 1989.

Films

Adventures of Tom Sawyer (Video). University Pictures, 1973. (76 minutes)

Adventures of Tom Sawyer (The Playhouse Video). 1988. (91 minutes)

Grapes of Wrath (the Video). Key Video, 1988. (129 minutes)

It's a Wonderful Life (Video). Republic Pictures, 1947. (160 minutes)

Tom Sawyer (Video). Reader's Digest, 1973. (102 minutes)

Software

Do-It-Yourself Lawyer. Expert Software, P.O. Box 144506, Coral Gable, FL 33114-4506. 1-305-567-9996.

In the First Degree. Broderbund. P.O. Box 6125, Novato, CA 94948—6125. 1-800-521-6263.

3-D Design Furniture. Expert Software, P.O. Box 144506, Coral Gable, FL 33114-4506. 1-305-567-9996.

Where in the USA Is Carmen Sandiego? Broderbund. P.O. Box 6125, Novato, CA 94948-6125.

Education Materials

Justice and Dissent. Prentice Hall, 1996.

Answer Key

Searching for Terms, page 17
1. plea bargain
2. fugitive
3. warrant
4. verdict
5. unconstitutional
6. trial
7. testimony
8. sustain
9. surveillance
10. suspect
11. subpoena
12. sentence
13. self-defense
14. negligence
15. objection
16. parole
17. fine
18. perjury
19. plea
20. search warrant

```
V E R D I C T E S T I M O N Y S
L A Y R U J R E P U E N P S E
C A E E S S A Z P T E X E L L
F U G I T I V E N G L I A L O
O U W P A R O C O I Q B O P
T R I A L D T O Q U E M E G R
U T E U A R T C E J I S
T W E R R A U S T E J B R T
I S U A R T S A C E B I U
T R A N T H P A F B I I N C
E N T E N C E K B I U T
N S U S T A I N A O V F
C O D D S U B P O E N A L Y H
E I W S F R E A G Q E P
N E G L I G E N C E A P A I J
U E C N A L L I E V R U S Z
```

Judicial Jargon—Level II, page 20
1. Bar Association
2. right to self-defense
3. plea bargaining
4. negligence
5. broke the case
6. suspect
7. defense attorney
8. evidence
9. witness
10. Judge
11. fugitive
12. examination
13. jury
14. parole
15. search warrant
16. sentence
17. trial
18. objection
19. verdict
20. perjury
21. bailiff
22. chambers
23. victim's
24. subpoena
25. prosecuting attorney
26. fine
27. incarcerated
28. coroner
29. cross examining

Using Your Terms, page 22
1. alibi
2. chambers
3. examination
4. bail
5. evidence
6. verdict
7. appeal
8. conviction
9. court
10. case
11. confession
12. contempt of court
13. crime
14. criminal
15. criminal action
16. Bar Association
17. breaking the case
18. case
19. affidavit
20. Civil action

Breaking the Law, page 25
Crimes: 1, 4, 6, 7, 9

Kids and Laws, page 26
1. vandalism
2. conversion
3. larceny
4. robbery
5. arson
6. burglary

Types of Crimes and Punishments, page 27
1. fine
2. probation
3. parole
4. felonies
5. conversion
6. infractions
7. misdemeanors
8. crimes
9. incarceration
10. capital punishment

(hiding place for rubies: false teeth)

Motive, Means, Opportunity, pages 34 and 35

Case #1
1. Motive: money, history of theft and violence
2. Means: Yes, he is described as "big and muscular." He has big teeth.
3. Opportunity: He lived in the neighborhood. He was identified by the girl and the probation officer.

Case #2
1. *Motive:* She prides herself on her collection of antiques.
2. *Means:* She owns a nice store.
3. *Opportunity:* She probably has access to transportation. The shop is in the area of the Bear's house.

People in the Courtroom, page 38
1. defense attorney
2. defendant
3. bailiff
4. jury
5. prosecuting attorney
6. legal secretary
7. judge
8. clerk of the court
9. witness

Courtroom Cutouts, page 39
A. Defendant
B. Defense Attorney
C. Prosecuting Attorney
D. Bailiff
E. Judge
F. Jury
G. Witness

Supreme Court Procedure, page 62
1. F
2. T
3. F
4. T
5. T
6. T
7. F
8. T
9. F
10. F

Southern Dialect, page 66
1. j
2. k
3. f
4. l
5. n
6. c
7. b
8. d
9. o
10. g
11. h
12. e
13. i
14. m
15. a

Mississippi Math, page 67
1. 35,000 bales of cotton, 70 boats
2. 400 cords of wood
3. 1,000 cords of wood
4. 100 cords of wood
5. 1,400 cords of wood
6. 5 days
7. 300 hours
8. 12 $\frac{1}{2}$ days
9. 900 cords of wood
10. 3,375 cords of wood

Ethics . . . In and Out of Court, page 70
Answers will vary.